THE CHILI-HOT
MEXICAN
COOKBOOK

THE CHILI-HOT
MEXICAN
COOKBOOK

SIZZLING DISHES FROM MEXICO, WITH 90 CLASSIC CHILI
RECIPES SHOWN STEP BY STEP IN OVER 390 PHOTOGRAPHS

JANE MILTON

southwater

This edition is published by Southwater, an imprint of Anness Publishing Ltd,
Hermes House, 88–89 Blackfriars Road, London SE1 8HA; tel. 020 7401 2077; fax 020 7633 9499
www.southwaterbooks.com; www.annesspublishing.com

If you like the images in this book and would like to investigate using them for publishing, promotions or
advertising, please visit our website www.practicalpictures.com for more information.

UK agent: The Manning Partnership Ltd; tel. 01225 478444; fax 01225 478440;
sales@manning-partnership.co.uk
UK distributor: Book Trade Services; tel. 0116 2759086; fax 0116 2759090;
uksales@booktradeservices.com; exportsales@booktradeservices.com
North American agent/distributor: National Book Network; tel. 301 459 3366; fax 301 429 5746;
www.nbnbooks.com
Australian agent/distributor: Pan Macmillan Australia; tel. 1300 135 113; fax 1300 135 103;
customer.service@macmillan.com.au
New Zealand agent/distributor: David Bateman Ltd; tel. (09) 415 7664; fax (09) 415 8892

Publisher: Joanna Lorenz
Executive Editor: Linda Fraser
Senior Editor: Joanne Rippin
Project Editor: Helen Marsh
Consultant Editor: Jenni Fleetwood
Designer: Nigel Partridge
Photography: Simon Smith (recipes) and Janine Hosegood (reference)
Food for Photography: Caroline Barty (recipes) and Annabel Ford (reference)

ETHICAL TRADING POLICY

Because of our ongoing ecological investment programme, you, as our customer, can have the pleasure and reassurance of knowing that
a tree is being cultivated on your behalf to naturally replace the materials used to make the book you are holding. For further information
about this scheme, go to www.annesspublishing.com/trees

Previously published as *Mexican Red Hot Cookbook*

NOTES

Bracketed terms are intended for American readers.

For all recipes, quantities are given in both metric and imperial measures and, where appropriate, measures are also given
in standard cups and spoons. Follow one set, but not a mixture, because they are not interchangeable.

Standard spoon and cup measures are level. 1 tsp = 5ml, 1 tbsp = 15ml, 1 cup = 250ml/8fl oz
Australian standard tablespoons are 20ml. Australian readers should use 3 tsp in place of
1 tbsp for measuring small quantities of gelatine, flour, salt etc.

Medium (US large) eggs are used unless otherwise stated.

Main front cover image shows Beef Enchiladas with Red Sauce – for recipe, see page 69.

PUBLISHER'S NOTE

Although the advice and information in this book are believed to be accurate and true at the time of going to press,
neither the authors nor the publisher can accept any legal responsibility or liability for any errors or omissions that may be made
nor for any inaccuracies nor for any harm or injury that comes about from following instructions or advice in this book.

CONTENTS

Introduction

Mexican food mirrors the culture of the country — it is colourful,
rich, stimulating and festive. From the wild and barren north to the
sultry heat of the south, this vast country offers the food lover
a feast of flavours. One of the distinguishing features of Mexican
cooking is the way it uses chillies as a central ingredient.
Chillies can be very hot indeed, but they can also impart a rich flavour
to food, and the recipes that follow introduce dishes that have
just a hint of heat as well as those that contain the great bursts of
flavourful fire that chilli-lovers seek.

Mexicans are experts at subtly blending flavours and taste
sensations so that each dish has its own unique character. If this is
your first introduction to genuine Mexican cuisine it will be a
revelation, and if you are already an aficionado then you will
find all you desire in these spicy and fiery recipes.

CHILLIES, FRESH AND DRIED

Chillies have been grown in South America for thousands of years. Over 150 indigenous varieties are found in Mexico alone. In 1492 Columbus took chillies to Europe, and from there they spread around the world.

Mexican food is often perceived as being very hot, and some of the dishes certainly live up to their reputation, but it is possible to find many dishes that are only mildly flavoured with chillies. The heat level of a chilli is determined by the amount of capsaicin it contains. This compound is concentrated mainly in the ribs and seeds, so you can reduce the fieriness considerably by removing these parts. Chillies that have been pickled, or that are used raw, tend to have more heat than cooked chillies.

Below: Jalapeño and serrano chillies

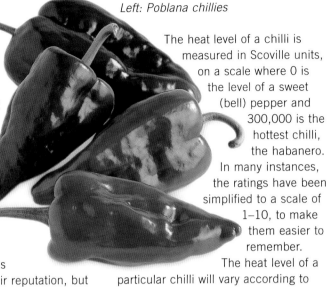

Left: Poblana chillies

The heat level of a chilli is measured in Scoville units, on a scale where 0 is the level of a sweet (bell) pepper and 300,000 is the hottest chilli, the habanero. In many instances, the ratings have been simplified to a scale of 1–10, to make them easier to remember.

The heat level of a particular chilli will vary according to where it was grown, when it was picked, the irrigation, the weather during the growing season and a host of other factors, so Scoville units can be only a guide. Each crop from the same plant will be different.

FRESH CHILLIES

The following are the most commonly used fresh chillies:

Serrano Heat level 8. This is a small chilli, about 4–5cm/1½–2in long and 1cm/½in wide, with a pointed tip. Serrano chillies change from green to red when ripe, and are sold at both stages of their development. The flavour is clean and biting. Serranos are used in cooked dishes, Guacamole and salsas.

Jalapeño Heat level 6. One of the most common – and most popular – types of chilli, this is about the same length as a serrano, but plumper. Jalapeños are sold at all stages of ripeness, so you are as likely to find red as green. Green jalapeños are often pickled. One method of preparing jalapeños is to stuff them with fresh cheese, coat in a light batter and deep-fry.

Poblano Heat level 3. Like many chillies, poblanos are initially green, and ripen to a dark red. They are large chillies, being roughly 8cm/3½in long

Roasting and Peeling Chillies

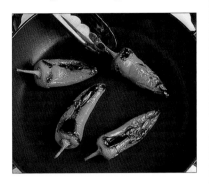

1 Dry-fry the chillies in a frying pan or griddle until the skins are scorched. Alternatively, spear them on a long-handled metal skewer and roast them over the flame of a gas burner until the skins blister and darken. Do not let the flesh burn.

2 Place the roasted chillies in a strong plastic bag and tie the top to keep the steam in. Set aside for 20 minutes.

3 Remove the chillies from the bag and peel off the skins. Cut off the stalks, then slit the chillies and scrape out the seeds.

Above: Fresno chillies

and 5.5cm/2¼in wide, and are sometimes said to be heart-shaped. Although not very hot, poblanos have a rich, earthy flavour which is intensified when the chillies are roasted and peeled. They are widely used in Mexican cooking, notably in Stuffed Chillies (*Chiles Rellenos*). Anaheim chillies, which are widely available in the United States and sometimes in the UK, can be substituted for poblanos.

Fresno Heat level 8. Looking rather like elongated sweet peppers, fresnos are about 6cm/2½in long and 2cm/¾in wide. They have a hot, sweet flavour and are used in salsas, as well as in meat, fish and vegetable dishes. They are particularly good in Black Bean Salsa and Guacamole.

Buying and Storing Fresh Chillies

Look for firm fresh chillies, with shiny skins. Try to avoid any specimens that are dull or limp, as they will be past their best. Fresh chillies can be successfully stored in a plastic bag in the refrigerator for up to 3 weeks. If they are to be chopped and added to cooked dishes, they can be seeded, chopped and then frozen, ready for use when required.

COOK'S TIP

If you bite into a chilli that is uncomfortably hot, swallow a spoonful of sugar. Don't be tempted to gulp down a glass of water or beer; this will only spread the heat further.

Preparing Fresh Chillies

Be very careful when handling fresh chillies as the capsaicin that they contain can cause severe irritation to sensitive skin, especially on the face. Either wear gloves when working with them, or wash your hands thoroughly with soap after handling them. If you touch your skin by mistake, wash your hands quickly and then splash the affected area with plenty of fresh cold water. Avoid scratching or rubbing inflamed skin, as this could aggravate the problem.

1 Holding the chilli firmly at the stalk end, cut it in half along its length with a sharp knife.

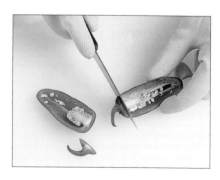

2 Cut off the stalk from both halves of the chilli, removing a thin slice of the top of the chilli as you do so. This will help to free the white membrane and make it easier to scrape out.

3 Carefully scrape out all of the seeds and remove the core with a small sharp knife.

4 Cut out any white membrane from the inside of the chillies. Keep the knife close to the flesh so that all the membrane is removed.

5 At this point make sure you carefully discard all of the seeds and membrane that are now lying on the board. Then take each half chilli and cut as required. To chop finely first cut the chilli half into thin strips. Then bunch the strips together and cut across them to produce tiny pieces. If the chilli is being added to a dish that will be cooked for some time, you can chop it less finely.

DRIED CHILLIES

Dried chillies are nothing new. The convenience of a product that could be stored and rehydrated when needed was realized centuries ago. Chillies were originally sun-dried, but today are more likely to be dried in an oven. Either way, they are a valuable ingredient, and are extensively used in this book because they are so much easier to obtain than fresh chillies are.

In many cases, drying intensifies the flavour of chillies. Depending on the process used, drying can also impart extra flavour, as when jalapeños are dried and smoked. Not only does the flavour deepen to a rich smokiness, but the name of the chilli changes, and it becomes a chipotle. The fact that the same chilli can have two names,

Above: Chilli powder

Above: Ancho chillies

Below: Cascabel chillies

depending on whether it is fresh or dried, can be confusing, and it may be simpler to think of dried chillies as separate varieties. The heat rating given for the dried chillies in the list that follows is based on the same scale as that used for the fresh chillies on the previous pages. Drying seems to spread the capsaicin through the chillies, so removing the seeds and membrane will do little to alter their heat. The seeds of a dried chilli add very little to the flavour, however, so if they are loose, discard them. Dried chillies can be ground to a powder or cut into strips before being used. Unless the chillies are to be added to a dish with a high proportion of liquid, they are usually soaked in water before use.

Buying and Storing Dried Chillies

Good quality dried chillies should be flexible, not brittle. Store them in an airtight jar in a cool, dry place. For short term storage, the refrigerator is ideal, although they can also be frozen. Do not keep dried chillies for more than a year or the flavour may depreciate.

The following is a list of some of the more common dried chillies, all of which feature in this book.

Ancho Heat scale 3. The most common dried chilli in Mexico, the ancho is a dried red poblano chilli, and has a fruity, slightly sharp flavour. When rehydrated, anchos can be used to make Stuffed Chillies (*Chiles Rellenos*), but should not be peeled first.

Cascabel Heat scale 4. The name means "little rattle" and refers to the noise that the seeds make inside the chilli. This chilli has a chocolate brown skin, and

Right: Chipotle chillies

Grinding Chillies

This method gives a distinctive and smoky taste to the resulting chilli powder.

1 Soak the chillies, pat dry and then dry-fry in a heavy pan until they are crisp.

2 Transfer to a mortar and grind to a fine powder with a pestle. Store in an airtight container.

remains dark, even after soaking. Cascabels have a slightly nutty flavour and are often added to salsas, such as *tomate verde*.

Chipotle Heat scale 6. These are smoked jalapeños. They add a

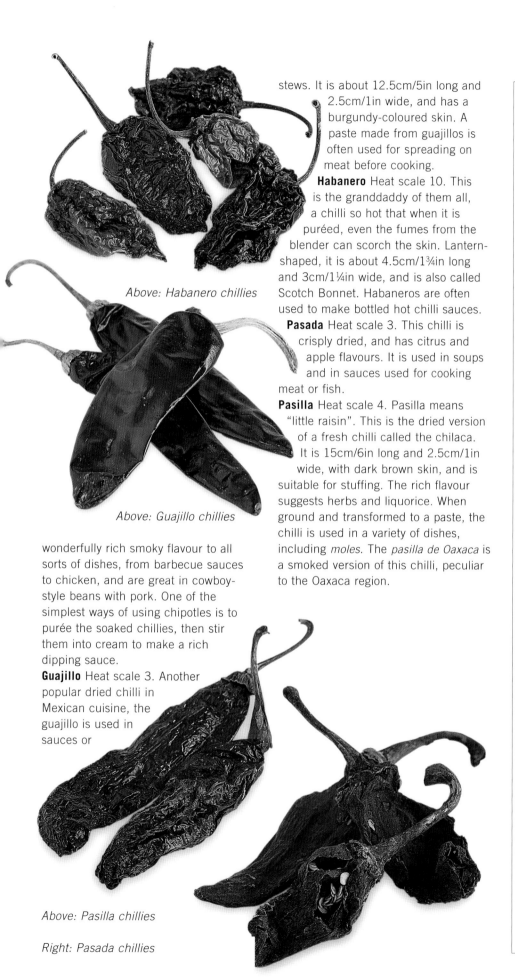

Above: Habanero chillies

Above: Guajillo chillies

wonderfully rich smoky flavour to all sorts of dishes, from barbecue sauces to chicken, and are great in cowboy-style beans with pork. One of the simplest ways of using chipotles is to purée the soaked chillies, then stir them into cream to make a rich dipping sauce.

Guajillo Heat scale 3. Another popular dried chilli in Mexican cuisine, the guajillo is used in sauces or

Above: Pasilla chillies

Right: Pasada chillies

stews. It is about 12.5cm/5in long and 2.5cm/1in wide, and has a burgundy-coloured skin. A paste made from guajillos is often used for spreading on meat before cooking.

Habanero Heat scale 10. This is the granddaddy of them all, a chilli so hot that when it is puréed, even the fumes from the blender can scorch the skin. Lantern-shaped, it is about 4.5cm/1¾in long and 3cm/1¼in wide, and is also called Scotch Bonnet. Habaneros are often used to make bottled hot chilli sauces.

Pasada Heat scale 3. This chilli is crisply dried, and has citrus and apple flavours. It is used in soups and in sauces used for cooking meat or fish.

Pasilla Heat scale 4. Pasilla means "little raisin". This is the dried version of a fresh chilli called the chilaca. It is 15cm/6in long and 2.5cm/1in wide, with dark brown skin, and is suitable for stuffing. The rich flavour suggests herbs and liquorice. When ground and transformed to a paste, the chilli is used in a variety of dishes, including *moles*. The *pasilla de Oaxaca* is a smoked version of this chilli, peculiar to the Oaxaca region.

Soaking Dried Chillies

In order to appreciate their full flavour, it is recommended that dried chillies which are not being ground should be soaked before being used. The amount of time chillies need to rehydrate depends on the type, the thickness of the skin and how dry they are. The longer they soak the better, so if there is time, leave them in the water for 1 hour before cooking.

1 Wipe them to remove any dirt, and brush away any seeds that are accessible.

2 Soak the dried chillies in a bowl of hot water for about 10 minutes (longer if possible) until the colour is restored and the chilli has swelled and softened.

3 Drain, cut off the stalks, then slit the chillies and scrape out the seeds with a small sharp knife. Slice or chop the flesh. If the chillies are to be puréed, put them in a blender or food processor with a little of the soaking water and process them until smooth.

SALSAS

Salsas have a varied role in Mexican cooking, they can be a cooling or refreshing accompaniment to a fiery hot dish perhaps, a soothing creamy sauce to go with some spicy meat, or they can be used to add crunch, heat or a bitter tang that contrasts with the main dish. This chapter includes salsas that will tantalize, soothe or scintillate the taste buds, using authentic Mexican ingredients such as chayote, jicama and nopales as well as the ever present and ever versatile chilli.

CLASSIC TOMATO SALSA

THIS IS THE TRADITIONAL TOMATO-BASED SALSA THAT MOST PEOPLE ASSOCIATE WITH MEXICAN FOOD. THERE ARE INNUMERABLE RECIPES FOR IT, BUT THE BASICS OF ONION, TOMATO, CHILLI AND CORIANDER ARE COMMON TO EVERY ONE OF THEM. SERVE THIS SALSA AS A CONDIMENT WITH A WIDE VARIETY OF DISHES.

SERVES SIX AS AN ACCOMPANIMENT

INGREDIENTS
   3–6 fresh serrano chillies
   1 large white onion
   grated rind and juice of 2 limes, plus
     strips of lime rind, to garnish
   8 ripe, firm tomatoes
   bunch of fresh coriander (cilantro)
   1.5ml/¼ tsp caster (superfine) sugar
   salt

1 Use 3 chillies for a salsa of medium heat; up to 6 if you like it hot. To peel the chillies spear them on a long-handled metal skewer and roast them over the flame of a gas burner until the skins blister and darken. Do not let the flesh burn. Alternatively, dry-fry them in a griddle pan until the skins are scorched.

2 Place the roasted chillies in a strong plastic bag and tie the top of the bag to keep the steam in. Set aside for about 20 minutes.

3 Meanwhile, chop the onion finely and put it in a bowl with the lime rind and juice. The lime juice will soften the onion.

VARIATIONS
Use spring onions (scallions) or mild red onions instead of white onion. For a smoky flavour, use chipotle chillies instead of fresh serrano chillies.

4 Remove the chillies from the bag and peel off the skins. Cut off the stalks, then slit the chillies and scrape out the seeds with a sharp knife. Chop the flesh coarsely and set aside.

5 Cut a small cross in the base of each tomato. Place the tomatoes in a heatproof bowl and pour in boiling water to cover.

6 Leave the tomatoes in the water for 3 minutes, then lift them out using a slotted spoon and plunge them into a bowl of cold water. Drain. The skins will have begun to peel back from the crosses. Remove the skins completely.

7 Dice the peeled tomatoes and put them in a bowl. Add the chopped onion which should have softened, together with the lime mixture. Chop the fresh coriander finely.

8 Add the coriander to the salsa, with the chillies and the sugar. Mix gently until the sugar has dissolved and all the ingredients are coated in lime juice. Cover and chill for 2–3 hours to allow the flavours to blend. The salsa will keep for 3–4 days in the refrigerator. Garnish with the strips of lime rind just before serving.

Green Tomatillo Sauce

This sauce, with its distinctive green colour and sharp taste, is a popular choice for pouring over enchiladas. When the cream is added, it is perfect for poached fish or with chicken breast portions. Fresh tomatillos are difficult to obtain outside Mexico, but the sauce can be made with canned tomatillos. Instructions for both versions are given here.

**SERVES FOUR AS A SAUCE
FOR A MAIN COURSE**

INGREDIENTS
  300g/11oz fresh tomatillos, plus
    120ml/4fl oz/½ cup stock or water
    or 300g/11oz drained canned
    tomatillos, plus 60ml/4 tbsp/¼ cup
    stock or water
  2 fresh serrano chillies
  4 garlic cloves, crushed
  15ml/1 tbsp vegetable oil
  bunch of fresh coriander (cilantro)
  120ml/4fl oz/½ cup double (heavy)
    cream (optional)
  salt

1 If using fresh tomatillos, remove the husks and cut the tomatillos into 4 pieces. Place them in a pan and add the stock or water. Cook over a moderate heat for 8–10 minutes until the flesh is soft and transparent.

2 Remove the stalks from the chillies, slit them and scrape out the seeds with a small knife. Chop the flesh coarsely and place it in a food processor or blender with the garlic.

3 Add the tomatillos to the processor or blender with their cooking liquid and process for a few minutes until almost smooth. If using drained canned tomatillos, simply cut into 4 and put in the blender or food processor with the smaller amount of stock or water and the chopped chillies and garlic. Process until almost smooth.

4 Heat the oil in a heavy frying pan and add the processed tomatillo purée. Reduce the heat and cook gently, stirring, for about 5 minutes until the sauce thickens. Be sure to keep stirring the sauce constantly, since it can easily catch and burn.

5 Chop the coriander and add it to the sauce, with salt to taste. Cook for a few minutes, stirring occasionally.

6 Stir in the cream, if using, and warm the sauce through. Do not let it boil. Serve immediately.

GUACAMOLE

ONE OF THE BEST LOVED MEXICAN SALSAS, THIS BLEND OF CREAMY AVOCADO, TOMATOES, CHILLIES, CORIANDER AND LIME NOW APPEARS ON TABLES THE WORLD OVER. BOUGHT GUACAMOLE USUALLY CONTAINS MAYONNAISE, WHICH HELPS TO PRESERVE THE AVOCADO, BUT THIS IS NOT AN INGREDIENT IN TRADITIONAL RECIPES.

SERVES SIX TO EIGHT

INGREDIENTS
    4 medium tomatoes
    4 ripe avocados, preferably fuerte
    juice of 1 lime
    ½ small onion
    2 garlic cloves
    small bunch of fresh coriander
        (cilantro), chopped
    3 fresh red fresno chillies
    salt
    tortilla chips, to serve

3 Cut the avocados in half then remove the stones (pits). Scoop the flesh out of the shells and place it in a food processor or blender. Process until almost smooth, then scrape into a bowl and stir in the lime juice.

4 Chop the onion finely, then crush the garlic. Add both to the avocado and mix well. Stir in the coriander.

5 Remove the stalks from the chillies, slit them and scrape out the seeds with a small sharp knife. Chop the chillies finely and add them to the avocado mixture, with the chopped tomatoes. Mix well.

6 Check the seasoning and add salt to taste. Cover with clear film (plastic wrap) or a tight-fitting lid and chill for 1 hour before serving with tortilla chips. Well covered, guacamole will keep in the refrigerator for 2–3 days.

1 Cut a cross in the base of each tomato. Place the tomatoes in a heatproof bowl and pour in boiling water to cover.

2 Leave the tomatoes in the water for 3 minutes, then lift them out using a slotted spoon and plunge them into a bowl of cold water. Drain. The skins will have begun to peel back from the crosses. Remove the skins completely. Cut the tomatoes in half, remove the seeds with a teaspoon, then chop the flesh coarsely and set it aside.

COOK'S TIP
Smooth-skinned fuerte avocados are native to Mexico, so would be ideal for this dip. If they are not available, use any avocados, but make sure they are ripe. To test, gently press the top of the avocado; it should give a little.

BLACK BEAN SALSA

THIS SALSA HAS A VERY STRIKING APPEARANCE. IT IS RARE TO FIND A BLACK SAUCE AND IT PROVIDES A WONDERFUL CONTRAST TO THE MORE COMMON REDS AND GREENS ON THE PLATE. THE PASADO CHILLIES ADD A SUBTLE CITRUS FLAVOUR. LEAVE THE SALSA FOR A DAY OR TWO AFTER MAKING TO ALLOW THE FLAVOURS TO DEVELOP FULLY.

SERVES FOUR AS AN ACCOMPANIMENT

INGREDIENTS

130g/4½oz/generous ½ cup black
   beans, soaked overnight in water
   to cover
1 pasado chilli
2 fresh red fresno chillies
1 red onion
grated rind and juice of 1 lime
30ml/2 tbsp Mexican beer (optional)
15ml/1 tbsp olive oil
small bunch of fresh coriander
   (cilantro), chopped
salt

1 Drain the beans and put them in a large pan. Pour in water to cover and place the lid on the pan. Bring to the boil, lower the heat slightly and simmer the beans for about 40 minutes or until tender. They should still have a little bite and should not have begun to disintegrate. Drain, rinse under cold water, then drain again and leave the beans until cold.

2 Soak the pasado chilli in hot water for about 10 minutes until softened. Drain, remove the stalk, then slit the chilli and scrape out the seeds with a small sharp knife. Chop the flesh finely.

COOK'S TIP
Mexican beer is widely exported nowadays, but if you can't find it, any light beer, can be substituted.

3 Spear the fresno chillies on a long-handled metal skewer and roast them over the flame of a gas burner until the skins blister and darken. Do not let the flesh burn. Alternatively, dry-fry them in a griddle pan until the skins are scorched. Then place the roasted chillies in a strong plastic bag and tie the top to keep the steam in. Set aside for 20 minutes.

4 Meanwhile, chop the red onion finely. Remove the chillies from the bag and peel off the skins. Slit them, remove the seeds and chop the flesh finely.

5 Tip the beans into a bowl and add the onion and both types of chilli. Stir in the lime rind and juice, beer, oil and coriander. Season with salt and mix well. Chill before serving.

PINTO BEAN SALSA

THESE BEANS HAVE A PRETTY, SPECKLED APPEARANCE. THE SMOKY FLAVOUR OF THE CHIPOTLE CHILLIES AND THE HERBY TASTE OF THE PASILLA CHILLI CONTRAST WELL WITH THE TART TOMATILLOS. UNUSUALLY, THESE ARE NOT COOKED.

2 Soak the chipotle and pasilla chillies in hot water for about 10 minutes until softened. Drain, reserving the soaking water. Remove the stalks, then slit each chilli and scrape out the seeds with a small sharp knife. Chop the flesh finely and mix it to a smooth paste with a little of the soaking water.

3 Roast the garlic in a dry frying pan over a moderate heat for a few minutes until the cloves start to turn golden. Crush them and add them to the beans.

SERVES FOUR AS AN ACCOMPANIMENT

INGREDIENTS
  130g/4½oz/generous ½ cup pinto beans, soaked overnight in water to cover
  2 chipotle chillies
  1 pasilla chilli
  2 garlic cloves, peeled
  ½ onion
  200g/7oz fresh tomatillos
  salt

1 Drain the beans and put them in a large pan. Pour in water to cover and place the lid on the pan. Bring to the boil, lower the heat slightly and simmer the beans for 45–50 minutes or until tender. They should still have a little bite and should not have begun to disintegrate. Drain, rinse under cold water, then drain again and tip into a bowl. Leave the beans until cold.

COOK'S TIP
Canned tomatillos can be substituted, but to keep a clean, fresh flavour add a little lime juice.

4 Chop the onion and tomatillos and stir them into the beans. Add the chilli paste and mix well. Add salt to taste, cover and chill before serving.

CHIPOTLE SAUCE

THE SMOKY FLAVOUR OF THIS SAUCE MAKES IT IDEAL FOR GRILLED FOOD, EITHER AS A MARINADE OR AS AN ACCOMPANIMENT. IT IS ALSO WONDERFUL STIRRED INTO CREAM CHEESE AS A SANDWICH FILLING WITH CHICKEN. CHIPOTLE CHILLIES ARE SMOKED DRIED JALAPEÑO CHILLIES.

SERVES SIX AS AN ACCOMPANIMENT

INGREDIENTS
  500g/1¼lb tomatoes
  5 chipotle chillies
  3 garlic cloves, coarsely chopped
  150ml/¼ pint/⅔ cup red wine
  5ml/1 tsp dried oregano
  60ml/4 tbsp clear honey
  5ml/1 tsp American mustard
  2.5ml/½ tsp ground black pepper
  salt

1 Preheat the oven to 200°C/400°F/ Gas 6. Cut the tomatoes into quarters and place them in a roasting pan. Roast for 45 minutes–1 hour, until they are charred and softened.

2 Meanwhile, soak the chillies in a bowl of cold water to cover for about 20 minutes or until soft. Remove the stalks, slit the chillies and scrape out the seeds with a small sharp knife. Chop the flesh coarsely.

3 Remove the tomatoes from the oven, let them cool slightly, then remove the skins. If you prefer a smooth sauce, remove the seeds. Chop the tomatoes and put them in a blender or food processor. Add the chopped chillies and garlic with the red wine. Process until smooth, then add the oregano, honey, mustard and black pepper. Process briefly to mix, then taste and season with salt.

4 Scrape the mixture into a small pan. Place over a moderate heat and stir until the mixture boils. Lower the heat and gently simmer the sauce, stirring occasionally, for about 10 minutes until it has reduced and thickened. Spoon into a bowl and serve hot or cold.

GUAJILLO CHILLI SAUCE

THIS SAUCE CAN BE SERVED OVER ENCHILADAS OR STEAMED VEGETABLES. IT IS ALSO GOOD WITH MEATS SUCH AS PORK, AND A LITTLE MAKES A FINE SEASONING FOR SOUPS OR STEWS. MADE FROM DRIED CHILLIES, IT HAS A WELL-ROUNDED, FRUITY FLAVOUR AND IS NOT TOO HOT.

SERVES FOUR AS AN ACCOMPANIMENT

INGREDIENTS
  2 tomatoes, total weight about
    200g/7oz
  2 red (bell) peppers, cored, seeded
    and cut into 4 pieces
  3 garlic cloves, in their skins
  2 ancho chillies
  2 guajillo chillies
  30ml/2 tbsp tomato purée (paste)
  5ml/1 tsp dried oregano
  5ml/1 tsp soft dark brown sugar
  300ml/½ pint/1¼ cups chicken stock

1 Preheat the oven to 200°C/400°F/ Gas 6. Cut the tomatoes into 4 pieces and place them in a roasting pan with the peppers and whole garlic cloves. Roast for 45 minutes–1 hour, until the tomatoes and peppers are slightly charred and the garlic has softened.

2 Put the peppers in a strong plastic bag and tie the top to keep the steam in. Set aside for 20 minutes. Remove the skin from the tomatoes. Meanwhile, soak the chillies in boiling water for 15 minutes until soft.

3 Remove the peppers from the bag and rub off the skins. Cut them in half, remove the cores and seeds, then chop the flesh coarsely and put it in a food processor or blender. Drain the chillies, remove the stalks, then slit them and scrape out the seeds with a sharp knife. Chop the chillies coarsely and add them to the peppers.

4 Add the roasted tomatoes to the food processor or blender. Squeeze the roasted garlic out of the skins and add to the tomato mixture, with the tomato purée, oregano, brown sugar and stock. Process until smooth.

5 Pour the mixture into a pan, place over a moderate heat and bring to the boil. Lower the heat and simmer for 10–15 minutes until the sauce has reduced to about half. Transfer to a bowl and serve immediately or, if serving cold, cover, leave to cool, then chill until required. The sauce will keep in the refrigerator for up to a week.

ROASTED TOMATO SALSA

SLOW ROASTING THESE TOMATOES TO A SEMI-DRIED STATE RESULTS IN A VERY RICH, FULL-FLAVOURED SWEET SAUCE. THE COSTENO AMARILLO CHILLI IS MILD AND HAS A FRESH LIGHT FLAVOUR, MAKING IT THE PERFECT PARTNER FOR THE RICH TOMATO TASTE. THIS SALSA IS GREAT WITH TUNA OR SEA BASS AND MAKES A MARVELLOUS SANDWICH FILLING WHEN TEAMED WITH CREAMY CHEESE.

SERVES SIX AS AN ACCOMPANIMENT

INGREDIENTS
500g/1¼lb tomatoes
8 small shallots
5 garlic cloves
sea salt
1 fresh rosemary sprig
2 costeno amarillo chillies
grated rind and juice of
  ½ small lemon
30ml/2 tbsp extra virgin olive oil
1.5ml/¼ tsp soft dark brown sugar

1 Preheat the oven to 160°C/325°F/ Gas 3. Cut the tomatoes into 4 pieces and place them on a baking tray.

2 Peel the shallots and garlic and add them to the roasting pan. Sprinkle with sea salt. Roast in the oven for 1¼ hours or until the tomatoes are beginning to dry. Do not let them burn or blacken or they will have a bitter taste.

3 Leave the tomatoes to cool, then peel off the skins and chop the flesh finely. Place in a bowl. Remove the outer layer of skin from any shallots that have toughened.

4 Using a large, sharp knife, chop the shallots and garlic coarsely, place them with the tomatoes in a bowl and mix.

5 Strip the rosemary leaves from the woody stem and chop them finely. Add half to the tomato and shallot mixture and mix lightly.

6 Soak the chillies in hot water for about 10 minutes until soft. Drain, remove the stalks, slit them and scrape out the seeds with a sharp knife. Chop the flesh finely and add it to the tomato mixture.

7 Stir in the lemon rind and juice, the olive oil and the sugar. Mix well, taste for seasoning and add more salt if needed. Cover and chill for at least an hour before serving, sprinkled with the remaining rosemary. It will keep for up to a week in the refrigerator.

COOK'S TIP
Use plum tomatoes or vine tomatoes, which have more flavour than tomatoes that have been grown for their keeping properties rather than their flavour. Cherry tomatoes make delicious roast tomato salsa and there is no need to peel them after roasting.

JICAMA SALSA

THE JICAMA IS A ROUND, BROWN ROOT VEGETABLE WITH A TEXTURE SOMEWHERE BETWEEN THAT OF WATER CHESTNUT AND CRISP APPLE. IT CAN BE EATEN RAW OR COOKED, AND IS ALWAYS PEELED. LOOK FOR JICAMAS IN ETHNIC FOOD STORES.

SERVES FOUR AS AN ACCOMPANIMENT

INGREDIENTS
　1 small red onion
　juice of 2 limes
　3 small oranges
　½ cucumber, cut lengthways
　1 fresh red fresno chilli
　1 *jicama*, about 450g/1lb

1 Cut the onion in half, then chop each half finely. Place in a bowl, add the lime juice and leave to soak while you prepare the oranges.

2 Slice the top and bottom off each orange. Stand an orange on a board, then carefully slice off all the peel and pith. Hold the orange over a bowl and cut carefully between the membranes so that the segments fall into the bowl. Having cut out all the segments, squeeze the pulp over the bowl to extract the remaining juice. Add the chopped onion to the bowl, with any remaining lime juice, and mix well.

COOK'S TIP
The juices of citrus fruits are very useful in preserving colour and freshness, and add more than flavouring to a recipe. For instance, lemon juice added to sliced apples keeps them white. Guacamole retains its colour for 2–3 days if lime juice is added to it. In this recipe the lime juice will slightly soften the finely chopped onion.

3 Use a teaspoon to scoop out the seeds from the cucumber half. Chop the cucumber into small pieces and set aside. Remove the stalk from the chilli, slit it and scrape out the seeds with a small sharp knife. Chop the flesh finely and set aside.

4 Peel the *jicama* and rinse it in cold water. Cut it into quarters, then slice finely. Add to the bowl of orange juice together with the cucumber and chilli. Mix well, then cover and leave to stand at room temperature for at least 1 hour before serving.

SWEET POTATO SALSA

VERY COLOURFUL AND DELIGHTFULLY SWEET, THIS SALSA MAKES THE PERFECT ACCOMPANIMENT TO HOT, SPICY MEXICAN DISHES.

SERVES FOUR AS AN ACCOMPANIMENT

INGREDIENTS
675g/1½lb sweet potatoes
juice of 1 small orange
5ml/1 tsp crushed dried
  jalapeño chillies
4 small spring onions (scallions)
juice of 1 small lime (optional)
salt

COOK'S TIP
This fresh and tasty salsa is also very good served with a simple grilled (broiled) salmon fillet or other fish dishes, and makes a delicious accompaniment to veal or grilled chicken.

1 Peel the sweet potatoes and dice the flesh finely. Bring a pan of water to the boil. Add the sweet potatoes and cook for 8–10 minutes, until just soft. Drain off the water, cover the pan and put it back on the hob (stovetop), having first turned off the heat. Leave the sweet potato for about 5 minutes to dry out, then tip into a bowl and set aside.

2 Mix the orange juice and crushed dried chillies in a bowl. Chop the spring onions finely and add them to the juice and chillies.

3 When the sweet potatoes are cool, add the orange juice mixture and toss carefully until all the pieces are thoroughly coated. Cover the bowl and chill for at least 1 hour, then taste and season with salt. Stir in the lime juice if you prefer a fresher taste. The salsa will keep for 2–3 days in a covered bowl in the refrigerator.

NOPALES SALSA

NOPALES ARE THE TENDER, FLESHY LEAVES OR "PADDLES" OF AN EDIBLE CACTUS KNOWN VARIOUSLY AS THE CACTUS PEAR AND THE PRICKLY PEAR CACTUS. THIS GROWS WILD IN MEXICO, BUT IS ALSO CULTIVATED. THE MOST FAMILIAR TYPE SOLD IN MEXICAN MARKETS HAS DARK GREEN OVALS WITH TINY THORNS. FRESH NOPALES ARE DIFFICULT TO TRACK DOWN OUTSIDE MEXICO, BUT IF YOU DO LOCATE A SUPPLY, LOOK FOR PADDLES THAT ARE FIRM AND SMOOTH SKINNED.

SERVES FOUR AS AN ACCOMPANIMENT

INGREDIENTS
    2 fresh red fresno chillies
    250g/9oz *nopales* (cactus paddles)
    3 spring onions (scallions)
    3 garlic cloves, peeled
    ½ red onion
    100g/3½oz fresh tomatillos
    2.5ml/½ tsp salt
    150ml/¼ pint/⅔ cup cider vinegar

1 Spear the chillies on a long-handled metal skewer and roast them over the flame of a gas burner until the skins blister and darken. Do not let the flesh burn. Alternatively, dry-fry them in a griddle pan until the skins are scorched. Place the roasted chillies in a strong plastic bag and tie the top to keep the steam in. Set aside for 20 minutes.

2 Remove the chillies from the bag and peel off the skins. Cut off the stalks, then slit the chillies and scrape out the seeds. Chop the chillies coarsely and set them aside.

COOK'S TIP
Fresh *nopales* are sometimes available from specialist fruit and vegetable stores. Like okra, they yield a sticky gum, and are best boiled before being used. Fresh cactus will lose about half its weight during cooking. Look out for canned *nopales* (sometimes sold as *nopalitos*) packed in water or vinegar.

3 Carefully remove the thorns from the nopales. Wearing gloves or holding each cactus paddle in turn with kitchen tongs, cut off the bumps that contain the thorns with a sharp knife.

4 Cut off and discard the thick base from each cactus paddle. Rinse the paddles well and cut them into strips, then cut the strips into small pieces.

5 Bring a large pan of lightly salted water to the boil. Add the cactus paddle strips, spring onions and garlic. Boil for 10–15 minutes, until the paddle strips are just tender.

6 Drain the mixture in a colander, rinse under cold running water to remove any remaining stickiness, then drain again. Discard the spring onions and garlic.

7 Chop the red onion and the tomatillos finely. Place in a bowl and add the cactus and chillies.

8 Spoon the mixture into a preserving jar, add the salt, pour in the vinegar and seal. Put the jar in the refrigerator for at least 1 day, turning the jar occasionally to ensure that the *nopales* are well marinated. The salsa will keep in the refrigerator for up to 10 days.

MANGO SALSA

THIS HAS A FRESH, FRUITY TASTE AND IS PERFECT WITH FISH OR AS A CONTRAST TO RICH, CREAMY DISHES. THE BRIGHT COLOURS MAKE IT AN ATTRACTIVE ADDITION TO ANY TABLE.

SERVES FOUR AS AN ACCOMPANIMENT

INGREDIENTS
    2 fresh red fresno chillies
    2 ripe mangoes
    ½ white onion
    bunch of fresh coriander (cilantro)
    grated rind and juice of 1 lime

1 To peel the chillies spear them on a long-handled metal skewer and roast them over the flame of a gas burner until the skins blister and darken. Do not let the flesh burn. Alternatively, dry-fry them in a griddle pan until the skins are scorched.

2 Place the roasted chillies in a strong plastic bag and tie the top to keep the steam in. Set aside for 20 minutes.

COOK'S TIP
Mangoes, in season, are readily available nowadays, but are usually sold unripe. Keep in a warm room for 24 hours or until they are just soft to the touch. Do not allow to ripen beyond this point.

3 Meanwhile, put one of the mangoes on a board and cut off a thick slice close to the flat side of the stone (pit). Turn the mango round and repeat on the other side. Score the flesh on each thick slice with criss-cross lines at 1cm/½in intervals, taking care not to cut through the skin. Repeat with the second mango.

4 Fold the mango halves inside out so that the mango flesh stands proud of the skin, in neat dice. Carefully slice these off the skin and into a bowl. Cut off the flesh adhering to each stone, dice it and add it to the bowl.

5 Remove the roasted chillies from the bag and carefully peel off the skins. Cut off the stalks, then slit the chillies and scrape out the seeds.

6 Chop the white onion and the coriander finely and add them to the diced mango. Chop the chilli flesh finely and add it to the mixture in the bowl, together with the lime rind and juice. Stir well to mix, cover and chill for at least 1 hour before serving. The salsa will keep for 2–3 days in the refrigerator.

ROASTED TOMATO AND CORIANDER SALSA

ROASTING THE TOMATOES GIVES A GREATER DEPTH TO THE FLAVOUR OF THIS SALSA, WHICH ALSO BENEFITS FROM THE WARM, ROUNDED FLAVOUR OF ROASTED CHILLIES.

SERVES SIX AS AN ACCOMPANIMENT

INGREDIENTS
    500g/1¼lb tomatoes
    2 fresh serrano chillies
    1 onion
    juice of 1 lime
    bunch of fresh coriander (cilantro)
    salt

1 Preheat the oven to 200°C/400°F/ Gas 6. Cut the tomatoes into 4 pieces and place them in a roasting pan. Add the chillies. Roast for 45 minutes–1 hour, until the tomatoes and chillies are charred and softened.

2 Place the roasted chillies in a strong plastic bag. Tie the top to keep the steam in and set aside for 20 minutes. Leave the tomatoes to cool slightly, then remove the skins and dice the flesh.

3 Chop the onion finely, then place in a bowl and add the lime juice and the chopped tomatoes.

4 Remove the chillies from the bag and peel off the skins. Cut off the stalks, then slit the chillies and scrape out the seeds with a sharp knife. Chop the chillies coarsely and add them to the onion mixture. Mix well.

5 Chop the coriander and add most to the salsa. Add salt, cover and chill for at least 1 hour before serving, sprinkled with the remaining coriander. This salsa will keep in the refrigerator for 1 week.

CHAYOTE SALSA

CHAYOTE — OR VEGETABLE PEAR, AS IT IS SOMETIMES CALLED — IS A GOURD-LIKE FRUIT, SHAPED LIKE A LARGE PEAR. SEVERAL VARIETIES GROW IN MEXICO, THE MOST COMMON BEING WHITE-FLESHED AND SMOOTH-SKINNED, WITH A TASTE REMINISCENT OF CUCUMBER. CHAYOTES SHOULD BE PEELED BEFORE BEING EATEN RAW OR COOKED. THE SEED, WHICH LOOKS RATHER LIKE A LARGE, FLAT ALMOND, IS EDIBLE. THE CONTRAST BETWEEN THE CRISP CHAYOTE, COOL MELON AND HOT HABANERO SAUCE MAKES THIS A SPECTACULAR SALSA.

SERVES SIX AS AN ACCOMPANIMENT

INGREDIENTS

1 *chayote*, about 200g/7oz
½ small Galia or ogen melon
10ml/2 tsp habanero sauce or similar
    hot chilli sauce
juice of 1 lime
2.5ml/½ tsp salt
2.5ml/½ tsp sugar

COOK'S TIP
In some countries, *chayotes* are called *christophenes* or *choko*. They are also used in Chinese cooking, so will be found in Asian stores.

1 Peel the *chayote*, then cut slices of flesh away from the stone (pit). Cut the slices into thin strips. Cut the melon in half, scoop the seeds out, and cut each half into 2 pieces. Remove the skin and cut the flesh into small cubes. Place in a bowl with the *chayote* strips.

2 Mix the chilli sauce, lime juice, salt and sugar in a bowl or jug (pitcher). Stir until all the sugar has dissolved. Pour over the melon and *chayote* mixture and mix thoroughly. Chill for at least 1 hour before serving. The salsa will keep for up to 3 days in the refrigerator.

PUMPKIN SEED SAUCE

THE ANCESTORS OF MODERN-DAY MEXICANS DIDN'T BELIEVE IN WASTING FOOD, AS THIS TRADITIONAL RECIPE PROVES. IT IS BASED UPON PUMPKIN SEEDS, THE FLESH HAVING BEEN USED FOR ANOTHER DISH, AND HAS A DELICIOUS NUTTY FLAVOUR. IT IS GREAT SERVED OVER STEAMED OR BOILED NOPALES (CACTUS PADDLES) AND IS ALSO DELICIOUS WITH CHICKEN OR RACK OF LAMB.

SERVES FOUR AS AN ACCOMPANIMENT

INGREDIENTS
  130g/4½oz/1 cup raw pumpkin seeds
  500g/1¼lb tomatoes
  2 garlic cloves, crushed
  300ml/½ pint/1¼ cups chicken
    stock, preferably freshly made
  15ml/1 tbsp vegetable oil
  45ml/3 tbsp red chilli sauce
  salt (optional)

1 Preheat the oven to 200°C/400°F/ Gas 6. Heat a heavy frying pan until very hot. Add the pumpkin seeds and dry-fry them, stirring constantly over the heat. The seeds will start to swell and pop, but they must not be allowed to scorch (see Cook's Tip). When all the seeds have popped, remove the pan from the heat.

2 Cut the tomatoes into 4 pieces and place them on a baking tray. Roast in the hot oven for 45 minutes–1 hour, until charred and softened. Allow to cool slightly, then remove the skins using a small sharp knife.

3 Put the pumpkin seeds in a food processor and process until smooth. Add the tomatoes and process for a few minutes, then add the garlic and stock and process for 1 minute more.

COOK'S TIP
When dry-frying the pumpkin seeds, don't stop stirring for a moment or they may scorch, which would make the sauce bitter. It is a good idea to stand back a little as some of the hot seeds may fly out of the pan.

4 Heat the oil in a large frying pan. Add the red chilli sauce and cook, stirring constantly, for 2–3 minutes. Add the pumpkin seed mixture and bring to the boil, stirring constantly.

5 Simmer for 20 minutes, stirring frequently until the sauce has thickened and reduced by about half. Taste and add salt, if needed. Serve over meat or vegetables or cool and chill. The salsa will keep for up to 7 days in a covered bowl in the refrigerator.

ONION RELISH

THIS POPULAR RELISH, KNOWN AS CEBOLLAS EN ESCABECHE, IS TYPICAL OF THE YUCATAN REGION AND IS OFTEN SERVED WITH CHICKEN, FISH OR TURKEY DISHES. TRY IT WITH CRACKERS AND CHEESE — IT ADDS A SPICY, TANGY TASTE AND WON'T CONTRIBUTE ANY ADDITIONAL FAT OR SUGAR.

MAKES ONE SMALL JAR

INGREDIENTS
2 fresh red fresno chillies
5ml/1 tsp allspice berries
2.5ml/½ tsp black peppercorns
5ml/1 tsp dried oregano
2 white onions
2 garlic cloves, peeled
100ml/3½fl oz/⅓ cup white
  wine vinegar
200ml/7fl oz/scant cup cider vinegar
salt

1 Spear the fresno chillies on a long-handled metal skewer and roast them over the flame of a gas burner until the skins blister. Do not let the flesh burn. Alternatively, dry-fry them in a griddle pan until the skins are scorched. Place the roasted chillies in a strong plastic bag and tie the top to keep the steam in. Set aside for 20 minutes.

2 Meanwhile, place the allspice, black peppercorns and oregano in a mortar or food processor. Grind slowly by hand with a pestle or process until coarsely ground.

3 Cut the onions in half and slice them thinly. Put them in a bowl. Dry-roast the garlic in a heavy frying pan over low heat until golden, then crush and add to the onions in the bowl.

4 Remove the chillies from the bag and peel off the skins. Slit the chillies, scrape out the seeds with a small sharp knife, then chop them.

COOK'S TIP
White onions have a pungent flavour and are good in this salsa, but other varieties of onions can also be used.

5 Add the ground spices to the onion mixture, followed by the chillies. Stir in both vinegars. Add salt to taste and mix thoroughly. Cover the bowl and chill for at least 1 day before use.

CHILLI STRIPS WITH LIME

THIS FRESH RELISH IS IDEAL FOR SERVING WITH STEWS, RICE DISHES OR BEAN DISHES. THE OREGANO ADDS A SWEET NOTE AND THE ABSENCE OF SUGAR OR OIL MAKES THIS A VERY HEALTHY CHOICE.

2 Meanwhile, slice the onion very thinly and put it in a large bowl. Squeeze the limes and add the juice to the bowl, with any pulp that gathers in the strainer. The lime juice will soften the onion. Stir in the oregano.

3 Remove the chillies from the bag and peel off the skins. Slit them, scrape out the seeds with a small sharp knife, then cut the chillies into long strips, which are called "rajas".

4 Add the chilli strips to the onion mixture and season with salt. Cover the bowl and chill for at least 1 day before serving, to allow the flavours to blend. The salsa will keep for up to 2 weeks in a covered bowl in the refrigerator.

MAKES ABOUT 60ML/4 TBSP

INGREDIENTS
   10 fresh green chillies
   ½ white onion
   4 limes
   2.5ml/½ tsp dried oregano
   salt

COOK'S TIP
This method of roasting chillies is ideal if you need more than 1 or 2, or if you do not have a gas burner. To roast over a burner, spear the chillies, 4 or 5 at a time, on a long-handled metal skewer and hold them over the flame until the skins blister.

1 Roast the chillies in a griddle pan over a moderate heat until the skins are charred and blistered. The flesh should not be allowed to blacken as this might make the salsa bitter. Place the roasted chillies in a strong plastic bag and tie the top to keep the steam in. Set aside for 20 minutes.

HABANERO SALSA

THIS IS A VERY FIERY SALSA WITH AN INTENSE HEAT LEVEL. A DAB ON THE PLATE ALONGSIDE A MEAT OR FISH DISH ADDS A FRESH, CLEAN TASTE, BUT THIS IS NOT FOR THE FAINT-HEARTED. HABANERO CHILLIES, ALSO CALLED SCOTCH BONNETS, ARE VERY HOT. LANTERN-SHAPED, THEY RANGE IN COLOUR FROM YELLOW TO A DEEP ORANGE RED. COSTEÑO AMARILLO CHILLIES ARE YELLOW WHEN FRESH AND HAVE A SHARP CITRUS FLAVOUR.

3 Put the chillies in a food processor and add a little of the soaking liquid. Process to a fine paste. Do not lean over the processor – the fumes may burn your face. Remove the lid and scrape the mixture into a bowl.

4 Put the chopped spring onions in another bowl and add the grapefruit juice, with the lime rind and juice. Coarsely chop the coriander.

SERVE SPARINGLY

INGREDIENTS
   5 dried roasted habanero chillies
   4 dried costeno amarillo chillies
   3 spring onions (scallions),
     finely chopped
   juice of ½ large grapefruit
   grated rind and juice of 1 lime
   bunch of fresh coriander (cilantro)
   salt

1 Soak the habanero and costeno amarillo chillies in hot water for about 10 minutes until softened. Drain, reserving the soaking water.

2 Wear rubber gloves to handle the habaneros. Remove the stalks from all chillies, then slit them and scrape out the seeds with a small sharp knife. Chop the chillies coarsely.

5 Add the coriander to the chilli mixture, then add the onion and mix thoroughly. Add salt to taste. Cover and chill for several hours. Serve sparingly.

ADOBO SEASONING

ADOBO MEANS VINEGAR SAUCE, AND THIS ADOBO IS A CHILLI VINEGAR PASTE USED FOR MARINATING PORK CHOPS OR STEAKS. ADOBOS ARE WIDELY USED IN THE COOKING OF THE YUCATÁN.

MAKES ENOUGH TO MARINATE
SIX CHOPS OR STEAKS

INGREDIENTS
   1 small head of garlic
   5 ancho chillies
   2 pasilla chillies
   15ml/1 tbsp dried oregano
   5ml/1 tsp cumin seeds
   6 cloves
   5ml/1 tsp coriander seeds
   10cm/4in piece of cinnamon stick
   10ml/2 tsp salt
   120ml/4fl oz/½ cup white
      wine vinegar

1 Preheat the oven to 180°C/350°F/ Gas 4. Cut a thin slice off the top of the head of garlic, so that the inside of each clove is exposed. Wrap the head of garlic in foil. Roast for 45–60 minutes or until the garlic is soft.

2 Meanwhile, slit the chillies and scrape out the seeds. Put the chillies in a blender or a mortar. Add the oregano, cumin seeds, cloves, coriander seeds, cinnamon stick and salt. Process or grind with a pestle to a fine powder.

3 Remove the garlic from the oven. When it is cool enough to handle, squeeze the garlic pulp out of each clove and grind into the spice mix.

4 Add the wine vinegar to the spice and garlic mixture and process or grind until a smooth paste forms. Spoon into a bowl and leave to stand for 1 hour, to allow the flavours to blend. Spread over pork chops or steaks as a marinade, before grilling (broiling) or cooking on the barbecue.

RED RUB

THIS "RUB" OR DRY PASTE IS FREQUENTLY USED IN THE YUCATÁN FOR SEASONING MEAT. THE MIXTURE IS RUBBED ON TO THE SURFACE OF THE MEAT, WHICH IS THEN WRAPPED IN BANANA LEAVES AND COOKED SLOWLY IN A PIB, A HEATED STONE-LINED HOLE IN THE GROUND. MEAT COOKED THIS WAY IS REFERRED TO AS PIBIL-STYLE. TRY USING THE RUB ON PORK CHOPS OR CHICKEN PIECES BEFORE OVEN BAKING OR COOKING ON THE BARBECUE.

MAKES ENOUGH FOR ONE JOINT OF MEAT
OR FOUR CHICKEN BREASTS

INGREDIENTS
    10ml/2 tsp achiote (annatto) seeds
    5ml/1 tsp black peppercorns
    5ml/1 tsp allspice berries
    5ml/1 tsp dried oregano
    2.5ml/½ tsp ground cumin
    5ml/1 tsp freshly squeezed lime juice
    1 small Seville (Temple) orange

1 Put the achiote seeds in a mortar and grind them with a pestle to a fine powder. Alternatively, use a food processor. Add the peppercorns, grind again, then repeat the process with the allspice berries. Mix in the oregano and ground cumin.

2 Add the lime juice to the spice mixture. Squeeze the orange and add the juice to the spice mixture, a teaspoonful at a time, until a thick paste is produced. Don't be tempted to substitute a sweet orange if Seville oranges are out of season; the spice mixture must be tart.

3 Allow the paste to stand for at least 30 minutes so the spices absorb the juice. The correct consistency for the paste is slightly dry and crumbly. When ready to use, rub the paste on to the surface of the meat, then leave to marinate for at least 1 hour before cooking, preferably overnight. The rub will keep for up to 7 days in a covered bowl in the refrigerator, after which time some of the flavour will be lost.

COOK'S TIP
Achiote is the rusty red seed of the annatto, a tropical American tree. It is used in Mexico for flavouring and colouring cheeses, butter and smoked fish. It is also used in Indian cooking and can be purchased from ethnic food stores.

RED SALSA

USE THIS AS A CONDIMENT WITH FISH OR MEAT DISHES, OR AS A DIPPING SAUCE FOR BAKED POTATO WEDGES. IT IS OFTEN ADDED TO RICE DISHES.

MAKES ABOUT 250ML/8FL OZ/1 CUP

INGREDIENTS
    3 large tomatoes
    15ml/1 tbsp olive oil
    3 ancho chillies
    2 pasilla chillies
    2 garlic cloves, peeled and left whole
    2 spring onions (scallions)
    10ml/2 tsp soft dark brown sugar
    2.5ml/½ tsp paprika
    juice of 1 lime
    2.5ml/½ tsp dried oregano
    salt

1 Preheat the oven to 200°C/400°F/ Gas 6. Cut the tomatoes into 4 pieces and place in a roasting pan. Drizzle over the oil. Roast for about 40 minutes until slightly charred, then remove the skin.

2 Soak the chillies in hot water for about 10 minutes. Drain, remove the stalks, slit and then scrape out the seeds. Chop the flesh finely. Dry roast the garlic in a heavy pan until golden.

3 Finely chop most of the spring onions, retaining the top part of 1 of them for garnishing. Place the chopped onion in a bowl with the sugar, paprika, lime juice and oregano. Slice the remaining spring onion diagonally and set aside for the garnish.

4 Put the peeled tomatoes and chopped chillies in a food processor or blender and add the garlic cloves. Process until smooth.

5 Add the sugar, paprika, lime juice, spring onions and oregano to the food processor or blender. Process for a few seconds, then taste and add salt as required. Spoon into a pan and warm through before serving, or place in a bowl, cover and chill until required. Garnish with the sliced spring onion. The salsa will keep, covered, for up to 7 days in the refrigerator.

Snacks

Mexicans love to snack. Street food is very popular throughout the country and in towns, cities and villages there will be stalls that sell fast food from barbecued corn to empanadas. These antojitos (little whims or nibbles) are also cooked in the home, for almuerzo, a kind of second breakfast served mid-morning, or merienda, a light supper that is usually eaten between 8 and 9pm. The recipes in this chapter are very versatile and can be used in a brunch, a light lunch, or a buffet supper, or you could serve a selection of them for a more substantial meal.

TLALPEÑO-STYLE SOUP

THIS SIMPLE CHICKEN SOUP ORIGINATES FROM TLALPAN, A SUBURB OF MEXICO CITY. THE SOUP IS MADE MORE SUBSTANTIAL BY THE ADDITION OF CHEESE AND CHICKPEAS.

SERVES SIX

INGREDIENTS
  1.5 litres/2½ pints/6¼ cups
    chicken stock
  ½ chipotle chilli, seeded
  2 skinless, boneless chicken
    breast portions
  1 medium avocado
  4 spring onions (scallions),
    thinly sliced
  400g/14oz can chickpeas, drained
  salt and ground black pepper
  75g/3oz/¾ cup grated Cheddar
    cheese, to serve

1 Pour the stock into a large pan and add the chilli. Bring to the boil, add the chicken, lower the heat and simmer for about 10 minutes or until the chicken is cooked. Remove the chicken from the pan and let it cool a little.

2 Using 2 forks, shred the chicken into small pieces. Set it aside. Pour the stock and chilli into a blender or food processor and process until smooth. Return the stock to the pan.

COOK'S TIP
When buying the avocado for this soup, choose one that is slightly under-ripe, which makes it easier to handle when peeling and slicing.

3 Cut the avocado in half, remove the skin and stone (pit), then slice the flesh into 2cm/¾in pieces. Add it to the stock, with the spring onions and chickpeas. Return the shredded chicken to the pan, with salt and pepper to taste, and heat gently.

4 Spoon the soup into heated bowls. Sprinkle grated cheese on top of each portion and serve immediately.

CORN SOUP

QUICK AND EASY TO PREPARE, THIS COLOURFUL SOUP HAS A SWEET AND CREAMY FLAVOUR. CHILDREN LOVE IT.

SERVES SIX

INGREDIENTS
  2 red (bell) peppers
  30ml/2 tbsp vegetable oil
  1 medium onion, finely chopped
  500g/1¼lb/3–4 cups sweetcorn
    kernels, thawed if frozen
  750ml/1¼ pints/3 cups chicken stock
  150ml/¼ pint/⅔ cup single
    (light) cream
  salt and ground black pepper

1 Dry-fry the peppers in a griddle pan over a moderate heat, turning them frequently until the skins are blistered all over. Place them in a strong plastic bag and tie the top to keep the steam in. Set aside for 20 minutes, then remove the peppers from the bag and peel off the skin.

2 Cut the peppers in half and scoop out the seeds and cores. Set 1 aside. Cut the other into 1cm/½in dice.

3 Heat the oil in a large pan. Add the onion and cook over a low heat for about 10 minutes, until it is translucent and soft. Stir in the diced pepper and sweetcorn and cook for 5 minutes over a moderate heat.

4 Spoon the contents of the pan into a food processor, pour in the chicken stock and process until almost smooth. This processing can be done in batches if necessary.

5 Return the soup to the pan and reheat it. Stir in the cream, with salt and pepper to taste. Core, seed and cut the reserved pepper into thin strips and add half of these to the pan. Serve the soup in heated bowls, garnished with the remaining pepper strips.

COOK'S TIP
Look for roasted red (bell) peppers in jars. These come ready-skinned and are useful in all sorts of recipes. Used here, they make a quick soup even speedier.

CHILES RELLENOS

STUFFED CHILLIES ARE POPULAR ALL OVER MEXICO. THE TYPE OF CHILLI USED DIFFERS FROM REGION TO REGION, BUT LARGER CHILLIES ARE OBVIOUSLY EASIER TO STUFF THAN SMALLER ONES. POBLANOS AND ANAHEIMS ARE QUITE MILD, BUT YOU CAN USE HOTTER CHILLIES IF YOU PREFER.

MAKES SIX

INGREDIENTS
6 fresh poblano or Anaheim chillies
2 potatoes, total weight 400g/14oz
200g/7oz/scant 1 cup cream cheese
200g/7oz/1¾ cups grated mature
  (sharp) Cheddar cheese
5ml/1 tsp salt
2.5ml/½ tsp ground black pepper
2 eggs, separated
115g/4oz/1 cup plain (all-
  purpose) flour
2.5ml/½ tsp white pepper
oil, for frying
chilli flakes, to garnish (optional)

1 Make a neat slit down 1 side of each chilli. Place them in a dry frying pan over a moderate heat, turning them frequently until the skins blister.

2 Place the chillies in a strong plastic bag and tie the top to keep the steam in. Set aside for 20 minutes, then carefully peel off the skins and remove the seeds through the slits, keeping the chillies whole. Dry the chillies with kitchen paper and set them aside.

COOK'S TIP
Take care when making the filling; mix gently, trying not to break up the potato pieces.

VARIATION
Whole ancho (dried poblano) chillies can be used instead of fresh chillies, but will need to be reconstituted in water before they can be seeded and stuffed.

3 Scrub or peel the potatoes and cut them into 1cm/½in dice. Bring a large pan of water to the boil, add the potatoes and let the water return to boiling point. Lower the heat and simmer for 5 minutes or until the potatoes are just tender. Do not overcook. Drain them thoroughly.

4 Put the cream cheese in a bowl and stir in the grated cheese, with 2.5ml/ ½ tsp of the salt and the black pepper. Add the potato and mix gently.

5 Spoon some of the potato filling into each chilli. Put them on a plate, cover with clear film (plastic wrap) and chill for 1 hour to firm the filling.

6 Put the egg whites in a clean, grease-free bowl and whisk them to firm peaks. In a separate bowl, beat the yolks until pale, then fold in the whites. Scrape the mixture on to a large, shallow dish. Spread out the flour in another shallow dish and season it with the remaining salt and the white pepper.

7 Heat the oil for frying to 190°C/ 375°F. Coat a few chillies first in flour and then in egg before adding carefully to the hot oil.

8 Fry the chillies in batches until golden and crisp. Drain on kitchen paper and serve hot, garnished with a sprinkle of chilli flakes for extra heat, if you like.

TORTAS

THE MULTI-LAYERED FILLING OF TORTAS OFFERS LOTS OF DIFFERENT TASTES AND TEXTURES.
TRADITIONALLY THEY ARE MADE USING ROLLS CALLED TELERAS.

SERVES TWO

INGREDIENTS
 2 fresh jalapeño chillies
 juice of ½ lime
 2 French bread rolls or 2 pieces
  of French bread
 115g/4oz/⅔ cup Refried Beans
 150g/5oz roast pork
 2 small tomatoes, sliced
 115g/4oz Cheddar cheese, sliced
 small bunch of fresh coriander
  (cilantro)
 30ml/2 tbsp crème fraîche

VARIATIONS

The essential ingredients of a *torta* are
refried beans and chillies. Everything
else is subject to change. Ham, chicken
or turkey could all be used instead of
pork, and lettuce is often added.

1 Cut the chillies in half, scrape out the
seeds, then cut the flesh into thin
strips. Put it in a bowl, pour over the
lime juice and leave to stand.

2 Slice the rolls or pieces of French
bread in half and remove some of the
crumb so that they are slightly
hollowed. Set the top of each piece of
roll or bread aside and spread the
bottom halves with the refried beans.

3 Cut the pork into thin shreds and put
these on top of the refried beans. Top
with the tomato slices. Drain the
jalapeño strips and put them on top of
the tomato slices. Add the cheese and
sprinkle with coriander leaves.

4 Turn the top halves of the rolls over,
so that the cut sides are uppermost,
and spread with crème fraîche.
Sandwich back together and and serve.

REFRIED BEANS

Refried beans are not actually fried
twice, but they are cooked twice, first as
Frijoles de Olla and then again by frying
in lard.

 To make this staple Mexican dish, cook
2 finely chopped onions in lard for about
30 minutes. When the onion has
caramelized add 5ml/1tsp ground cumin
and 5ml/1tsp ground coriander. Then
take one quantity Frijoles de Olla, and
add to the pan a spoonful at a time. As
they heat through mash them into the
onion mixture using a fork or a potato
masher. Continue until all the beans
have been added, then stir in 3 crushed
cloves of garlic.

 Lower the heat and cook the beans
until they form a thick paste. Season
with salt and pepper.

 Refried beans can be eaten as one of
the side dishes for tortillas together with
guacamole and sour cream.

TAQUITOS WITH BEEF

MINIATURE SOFT CORN TORTILLAS ARE MOULDED AROUND A TASTY FILLING AND SERVED WARM. UNLESS YOU HAVE ACCESS TO MINIATURE FRESH CORN TORTILLAS, YOU WILL NEED A TORTILLA PRESS.

2 Mix the *masa harina* and salt in a bowl. Add the water, a little at a time, to make a dough that can be worked into a ball. Knead this on a lightly floured surface for 3–4 minutes until smooth. Wrap the dough in clear film (plastic wrap) and leave to rest for 1 hour.

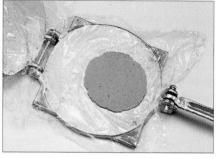

3 Divide the dough into 12 small balls. Open a tortilla press and line both sides with plastic (this can be cut from a new plastic sandwich bag). Put a ball on the press and bring the top down to flatten it into a 5–6cm/2–2½in round. Flatten the remaining dough balls in the same way to make more tortillas.

4 Heat a griddle or frying pan until hot. Cook each tortilla for 15–20 seconds on each side, and then for 15 minutes more on the first side. Keep the tortillas warm and soft by folding them inside a slightly damp dish towel.

5 Add the oregano, cumin, tomato purée and caster sugar to the pan containing the reserved beef cubes, with a couple of tablespoons of the reserved beef stock, or just enough to keep the mixture moist. Cook gently for a few minutes to combine the flavours.

6 Place a little of the lettuce on a warm tortilla. Top with a little of the filling and a little onion relish, fold in half and serve while still warm. Fill more tortillas in the same way.

SERVES TWELVE

INGREDIENTS
    500g/1¼lb rump (round) steak, diced
      into 1cm/½in pieces
    2 garlic cloves, peeled and left whole
    750ml/1¼ pints/3 cups beef stock
    150g/5oz/1 cup *masa harina*
    pinch of salt
    120ml/4fl oz/½ cup warm water
    7.5ml/1½ tsp dried oregano
    2.5ml/½ tsp ground cumin
    30ml/2 tbsp tomato purée (paste)
    2.5ml/½ tsp caster (superfine) sugar
    salt and ground black pepper
    shredded lettuce and Onion Relish,
      to serve

1 Put the beef and whole garlic cloves in a large pan and cover with the beef stock. Bring to the boil, lower the heat and simmer for 10–15 minutes, until the meat is tender. Using a slotted spoon, transfer the meat to a clean pan and set it aside. Reserve the stock.

EMPANADAS WITH ROPA VIEJA

THE FILLING FOR THESE EMPANADAS IS TRADITIONALLY MADE WITH MEAT THAT IS COOKED UNTIL IT IS SO TENDER THAT IT CAN BE TORN APART WITH FORKS. IT RESEMBLES TATTERED CLOTH, WHICH IS HOW IT CAME TO BE KNOWN AS ROPA VIEJA, WHICH MEANS "OLD CLOTHES".

SERVES SIX (TWELVE EMPANADAS)

INGREDIENTS

    150g/5oz/1 cup *masa harina*
    30ml/2 tbsp plain (all-purpose) flour
    2.5ml/½ tsp salt
    120–150ml/4–5fl oz/½–⅔ cup
      warm water
    15ml/1 tbsp oil, plus extra for frying
    250g/9oz lean minced (ground) pork
    1 garlic clove, crushed
    3 tomatoes
    2 ancho chillies
    ½ small onion
    2.5ml/½ tsp ground cumin
    tsp salt

1 Mix the *masa harina*, plain flour and salt in a bowl. Gradually add enough of the warm water to make a smooth, but not sticky dough. Knead briefly, then shape into a ball, wrap in clear film (plastic wrap) and set aside.

2 Heat 15ml/1 tbsp oil in a pan. Add the minced pork and cook, stirring frequently, until it has browned evenly. Stir in the garlic and cook for 2 minutes more. Remove from the heat and set the pan aside.

3 Cut a cross in the base of each tomato, place them in a bowl and pour over boiling water. After 3 minutes plunge the tomatoes into a bowl of cold water. Drain. The skins will peel back easily from the crosses. Remove the skins completely. Chop the tomato flesh and put in a bowl.

4 Slit the ancho chillies and scrape out the seeds. Chop the chillies finely and add them to the tomatoes. Chop the onion finely and add it to the tomato mixture, with the ground cumin.

5 Stir the tomato mixture into the pan containing the pork and cook over a moderate heat for 10 minutes, stirring occasionally. Season with salt to taste.

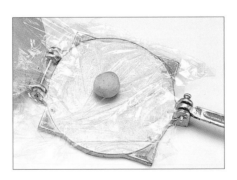

6 To make the tortillas, divide the empanada dough into 12 pieces and roll each piece into a ball. Open a tortilla press and line both sides with plastic (this can be cut from a new plastic sandwich bag). Put a ball of dough on the press and bring the top down to flatten it into a 7.5cm/3in round. Use the remaining dough balls to make more tortillas in the same way.

COOK'S TIP
If the empanada dough proves difficult to handle, a little oil or melted lard (shortening) can be kneaded into the dough to help make it more pliable.

7 Spoon a little of the meat mixture on half of each tortilla, working quickly to prevent the dough from drying out. Dampen the edges of the dough with a little water and fold, turnover-style, to make the empanadas.

8 Seal the edges on the empanadas by pinching them between the index finger and thumb of the left hand and the index finger of the right hand.

9 Heat a little oil in a large frying pan. When it is hot, fry the empanadas in batches until crisp and golden on both sides, turning at least once. Serve hot or cold.

QUESADILLAS

These cheese-filled tortillas are the Mexican equivalent of toasted sandwiches. Serve them as soon as they are cooked, or they will become chewy. If you are making them for a crowd, fill and fold the tortillas ahead of time, but only cook them to order.

SERVES FOUR

INGREDIENTS
  200g/7oz mozzarella, Monterey Jack
    or mild Cheddar cheese
  1 fresh fresno chilli (optional)
  8 wheat flour tortillas, about
    15cm/6in across
  Onion Relish or Classic Tomato Salsa,
    to serve

VARIATIONS
Try spreading a thin layer of your favourite Mexican salsa on the tortilla before adding the cheese, or adding a few pieces of cooked chicken or prawns (shrimp) before folding the tortilla.

1 If using mozzarella cheese, it must be drained thoroughly and then patted dry and sliced into thin strips. Monterey Jack and Cheddar cheese should both be coarsely grated, as finely grated cheese will melt and ooze away when cooking. Set the cheese aside in a bowl.

2 If using the chilli, spear it on a long-handled metal skewer and roast it over the flame of a gas burner until the skin blisters and darkens. Do not let the flesh burn. Alternatively, dry-fry it in a griddle pan until the skin is scorched. Place the roasted chilli in a strong plastic bag and tie the top to keep the steam in. Set aside for 20 minutes.

3 Remove the chilli from the bag and peel off the skin. Cut off the stalk, then slit the chilli and scrape out the seeds. Cut the flesh into 8 thin strips.

4 Warm a large frying pan or griddle. Place 1 tortilla on the pan or griddle at a time, sprinkle about an eighth of the cheese on to 1 half and add a strip of chilli, if using. Fold the tortilla over the cheese and press the edges together gently to seal. Cook the filled tortilla for 1 minute, then turn over and cook the other side for 1 minute.

5 Remove the filled tortilla from the pan or griddle, cut it into 3 triangles or 4 strips and serve immediately, with the onion relish or tomato salsa.

MEXICAN RICE

VERSIONS OF THIS DISH – A RELATIVE OF SPANISH RICE – ARE POPULAR ALL OVER SOUTH AMERICA.
CLASSIFIED AS A SOPA SECA *OR DRY SOUP, IT IS A DELICIOUS MEDLEY OF RICE, TOMATOES AND*
AROMATIC FLAVOURINGS. RATHER THAN WATER, THE LIQUID USED TO COOK THE RICE IS CHICKEN
STOCK AND TOMATO JUICE, GIVING THE DISH A RICH FLAVOUR.

SERVES SIX

INGREDIENTS
   200g/7oz/1 cup long grain rice
   200g/7oz can chopped tomatoes in
     tomato juice
   ½ onion, roughly chopped
   2 garlic cloves, roughly chopped
   30ml/2 tbsp vegetable oil
   450ml/¾ pint/scant 2 cups
     chicken stock
   2.5ml/½ tsp salt
   3 fresh fresno chillies or other fresh
     green chillies, trimmed
   150g/5oz/generous 1 cup frozen peas
   ground black pepper

1 Put the rice in a heatproof bowl and pour in boiling water to cover. Stir once, then set aside for 10 minutes. Tip into a strainer, rinse under cold water, then drain again. Set aside to dry slightly.

2 Meanwhile, pour the tomatoes and juice into a food processor or blender, add the onion and garlic and process until smooth.

3 Heat the oil in a large, heavy pan, add the rice and cook over a moderate heat until it becomes a delicate golden brown. Stir occasionally to ensure that the rice does not stick to the bottom of the pan.

4 Add the tomato mixture and stir over a moderate heat until all the liquid has been absorbed. Stir in the stock, salt, whole chillies and peas. Continue to cook the mixture, stirring occasionally, until all the liquid has been absorbed and the rice is just tender.

5 Remove the pan from the heat, cover it with a tight-fitting lid and leave it to stand in a warm place for 5–10 minutes. Remove the chillies, fluff up the rice lightly and serve, sprinkled with black pepper. The chillies may be used as a garnish, if you like.

COOK'S TIP
Do not stir the rice too often after adding the stock or the grains will break down and the mixture will become starchy.

CHICKEN FLAUTAS

CRISP FRIED TORTILLAS WITH A CHICKEN AND CHEESE FILLING MAKE A DELICIOUS LIGHT MEAL, ESPECIALLY WHEN SERVED WITH A SPICY TOMATO SALSA. THE SECRET OF SUCCESS IS TO MAKE SURE THAT THE OIL IS SUFFICIENTLY HOT TO PREVENT THE FLUTES FROM ABSORBING TOO MUCH OF IT.

MAKES TWELVE

INGREDIENTS
  2 skinless, boneless chicken
    breast portions
  1 onion
  2 garlic cloves
  15ml/1 tbsp vegetable oil
  90g/3½oz feta cheese, crumbled
  12 corn tortillas
  oil, for frying
  salt and ground black pepper
For the salsa
  3 tomatoes, peeled, seeded
    and chopped
  juice of ½ lime
  small bunch of fresh coriander
    (cilantro), chopped
  ½ small onion, finely chopped
  3 fresh fresno chillies or similar
    fresh green chillies, seeded
    and chopped

1 Start by making the salsa. Mix the tomatoes, lime juice, coriander, onion and chillies in a bowl. Season with salt to taste and set aside.

COOK'S TIP
You might find it easier to keep the cocktail sticks or toothpicks in place until after the flutes have been fried, in which case remove them before serving.

2 Put the chicken breast portions in a large pan, add water to cover and bring to the boil. Lower the heat and simmer for 15–20 minutes or until the chicken is cooked. Remove the chicken from the pan and let it cool a little. Using 2 forks, shred the chicken into small pieces. Set it aside.

3 Chop the onion finely and crush the garlic. Heat the oil in a frying pan, add the onion and garlic and cook over a low heat for about 5 minutes, or until the onion has softened but not coloured. Add the chicken, with salt and pepper to taste. Mix well, remove from the heat and stir in the feta.

4 Before they can be rolled, soften the tortillas by steaming 3 or 4 at a time on a plate over boiling water for a few moments until they are pliable. Alternatively, wrap them in microwave-safe film and then heat them in a microwave oven on full power for about 30 seconds.

5 Place a spoonful of the chicken filling on 1 tortilla. Roll the tortilla tightly around the filling to make a cylinder. Secure with a cocktail stick or toothpick. Immediately cover the roll with clear film (plastic wrap) to prevent the tortilla from drying out. Fill and roll the remaining tortillas in the same way.

6 Pour oil into a frying pan to a depth of 2.5cm/1in. Heat it until a small cube of bread, added to the oil, rises to the surface and bubbles at the edges before turning golden. Remove the cocktail sticks, then add the flutes to the pan, a few at a time.

7 Fry the flutes for 2–3 minutes until golden, turning frequently. Drain on kitchen paper and serve immediately, with the salsa.

EGGS <u>WITH</u> CHORIZO

IN MEXICO, THERE ARE TWO TYPES OF CHORIZO SAUSAGE. THE FIRST IS FRESHLY MADE AND SOLD LOOSE; THE SECOND IS PACKED IN SAUSAGE SKINS AND AIR-DRIED, LIKE SPANISH CHORIZO. THIS IS A RECIPE FOR THE FORMER. FRESHLY MADE CHORIZO CAN BE USED IN A NUMBER OF SAVOURY DISHES, BUT IS PARTICULARLY GOOD WITH SCRAMBLED EGGS, AS HERE.

SERVES FOUR

INGREDIENTS
25g/1oz/2 tbsp lard (shortening)
500g/1¼lb minced (ground) pork
3 garlic cloves, crushed
10ml/2 tsp dried oregano
5ml/1 tsp ground cinnamon
2.5ml/½ tsp ground cloves
2.5ml/½ tsp ground black pepper
30ml/2 tbsp dry sherry
5ml/1 tsp caster (superfine) sugar
5ml/1 tsp salt
6 eggs
2 tomatoes, peeled, seeded and
  finely diced
½ small onion, finely chopped
60ml/4 tbsp milk or single
  (light) cream
fresh oregano sprigs, to garnish
warm corn or wheat flour tortillas,
  to serve

1 Melt the lard in a large frying pan over a moderate heat. Add the pork and cook until browned, stirring frequently. Stir in the garlic, dried oregano, cinnamon, cloves and black pepper. Cook for 3–4 minutes more.

2 Add the sherry, sugar and salt to the frying pan, stir well and cook for 3–4 minutes until the flavours are blended. Remove from the heat.

3 Put the eggs in a bowl. Beat lightly to mix, then stir in the finely diced tomatoes and chopped onion.

4 Return the chorizo mixture to the heat. Heat it through and pour in the egg mixture. Cook, stirring constantly, until the egg is almost firm.

5 Stir in the milk or cream and check the seasoning. Garnish with fresh oregano and serve with warm corn or wheat flour tortillas.

CHILLIES <u>IN</u> CHEESE SAUCE

THIS MAKES AN EXCELLENT APPETIZER, LIGHT LUNCH OR DIP TO SERVE WITH DRINKS. THE CHILLIES AND TEQUILA GIVE IT QUITE A KICK.

SERVES FOUR TO SIX

INGREDIENTS
4 fresh fresno chillies
15ml/1 tbsp vegetable oil
½ red onion, finely chopped
500g/1¼lb/5 cups grated Monterey
  Jack cheese
30ml/2 tbsp crème fraîche
150ml/¼ pint/⅔ cup double
  (heavy) cream
2 firm tomatoes, peeled
15ml/1 tbsp reposada tequila
tortilla chips, to serve

COOK'S TIP
Cross-cut the base of a tomato and cover with boiling water. Plunge into cold water and the skin will peel easily.

1 Place the chillies in a dry frying pan over a moderate heat, turning them frequently until the skin blisters and darkens. Place the chillies in a strong plastic bag and tie the top to keep the steam in. Set aside for 20 minutes, then carefully peel off the skins. Slit the chillies and scrape out the seeds, then cut the flesh into thin strips. Cut these in half along their length.

2 Heat the oil in a frying pan and cook the onion over a moderate heat for 5 minutes, until it is beginning to soften. Add the cheese, crème fraîche and cream. Stir over a low heat until the cheese melts and the mixture becomes a rich, creamy sauce. Stir in the thin chilli strips.

3 Cut the tomatoes in half and scrape out the seeds. Cut the flesh into 1cm/½in pieces and stir these into the sauce.

4 Just before serving, stir in the tequila. Pour the sauce into a serving dish and serve warm, with the tortilla chips.

MOLETTES

THIS IS THE MEXICAN VERSION OF BEANS ON TOAST. SOLD BY STREET TRADERS AROUND MID-MORNING, THEY MAKE THE PERFECT SNACK FOR THOSE WHO HAVE MISSED BREAKFAST.

SERVES FOUR

INGREDIENTS
    4 crusty finger rolls
    50g/2oz/¼ cup butter, softened
    225g/8oz/1⅓ cups Refried Beans
    150g/5oz/1¼ cups grated medium
        Cheddar cheese
    green salad leaves, to garnish
    120ml/4fl oz/½ cup Classic Tomato
        Salsa, to serve

1 Cut the rolls in half, then take a sliver off the base so that they lie flat. Remove a little of the crumb. Spread them lightly with butter.

2 Arrange them on a baking sheet and grill (broil) for about 5 minutes, or until they are crisp and golden. Meanwhile, heat the refried beans over a low heat in a small pan.

3 Scoop the beans into the rolls, then sprinkle the grated cheese on top. Return to the grill (broiler) until the cheese melts. Serve with the tomato salsa and garnish with salad leaves.

EGGS MOTULENOS

A TASTY AND FILLING BREAKFAST OR MIDDAY SNACK, BLACK BEANS, WHICH ARE ALSO KNOWN AS TURTLE BEANS, ARE TOPPED WITH EGGS AND CHILLI SAUCE AND SURROUNDED BY PEAS AND HAM.

SERVES FOUR

INGREDIENTS
    225g/8oz/generous 1 cup black
        beans, soaked overnight in water
    1 small onion, finely chopped
    2 garlic cloves
    small bunch of fresh coriander,
        (cilantro) chopped
    150g/5oz/generous 1 cup frozen peas
    4 corn tortillas
    30ml/2 tbsp oil
    4 eggs
    150g/5oz cooked ham, diced
    60ml/4 tbsp hot chilli sauce
    75g/3oz feta cheese, crumbled
    salt and ground black pepper
    Classic Tomato Salsa, to serve

1 Drain the beans, rinse them under cold water and drain again. Put them in a pan, add the onion and garlic and water to cover. Bring to the boil, then simmer for 40 minutes. Drain the beans, stir in the coriander, with salt and pepper to taste, and keep hot.

2 Cook the peas in a small pan of boiling water until they are just tender. Drain and set aside. Wrap the tortillas in foil and place them on a plate. Stand the plate over a pan of boiling water and steam them for about 5 minutes. Alternatively, wrap them in microwave-safe film and heat them in a microwave on full power for about 30 seconds.

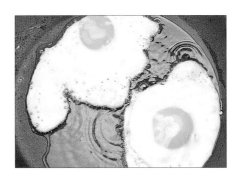

3 Heat the oil in a frying pan and fry the eggs until the whites are set. Lift them on to a plate and keep them warm while you quickly heat the ham and peas in the oil remaining in the pan.

4 Place the tortillas on warmed plates and top each of them with some beans. Place an egg on each tortilla, spoon 15ml/1 tbsp hot chilli sauce over the top, then surround each egg with some peas and ham. Sprinkle feta over the peas and serve immediately, with salsa on the side.

EGGS RANCHEROS

THERE ARE MANY VARIATIONS ON THIS POPULAR DISH, WHICH IS GREAT FOR BREAKFAST OR BRUNCH. THE COMBINATION OF CREAMY EGGS WITH ONION, CHILLI AND TOMATOES WORKS WONDERFULLY WELL.

SERVES FOUR FOR BREAKFAST

INGREDIENTS

2 corn tortillas, several days old
oil, for frying
2 fresh green jalapeño chillies
1 garlic clove
4 spring onions (scallions)
1 large tomato
8 eggs, beaten
150ml/¼ pint/⅔ cup single
   (light) cream
small bunch of fresh coriander
   (cilantro), finely chopped
salt and ground black pepper

1 Cut the tortillas into long strips. Pour oil into a frying pan to a depth of 1cm/½in. Heat until very hot, watching closely.

2 Fry the tortilla strips in batches for 1–2 minutes until they are crisp and golden, turning them occasionally, then drain on kitchen paper.

COOK'S TIP
When cooking the tortilla strips it is important that the oil is the correct temperature. To test if the oil is ready to use, carefully add a strip of tortilla. If the strip floats and the oil immediately bubbles around its edges, the oil is ready.

3 Spear the chillies on a long-handled metal skewer and roast them over the flame of a gas burner until the skins blister and darken. Do not let the flesh burn. Alternatively, dry-fry them in a griddle pan until the skins are scorched. Place them in a strong plastic bag and tie the top to keep the steam in. Set aside for 20 minutes.

4 Meanwhile, crush the garlic and chop the spring onions finely. Cut a cross in the base of the tomato. Place it in a heatproof bowl and pour over boiling water to cover. After 3 minutes lift the tomato out using a slotted spoon and plunge it into a bowl of cold water. Leave for a few minutes to cool.

5 Drain the tomato, remove the skin and cut it into 4 pieces. Using a teaspoon scoop out the seeds and the core, then dice the flesh finely.

6 Remove the chillies from the bag and peel off the skins. Cut off the stalks, then slit the chillies and scrape out the seeds. Chop the flesh finely. Put the eggs in a bowl, season with salt and pepper and beat lightly.

7 Heat 15ml/1 tbsp oil in a large frying pan. Add the garlic and spring onions and cook gently for 2–3 minutes until soft. Stir in the diced tomato and cook for 3–4 minutes more, then stir in the chillies and cook for 1 minute.

8 Pour the eggs into the pan and stir until they start to set. When only a small amount of uncooked egg remains visible, stir in the cream so that the cooking process is slowed down and the mixture cooks to a creamy consistency rather than a solid mass.

9 Stir the chopped coriander into the scrambled egg. Arrange the tortilla strips on 4 serving plates and spoon the eggs on top. Serve immediately.

SPICED PLANTAIN CHIPS

PLANTAINS ARE MORE STARCHY THAN THE BANANAS TO WHICH THEY ARE RELATED, AND MUST BE COOKED BEFORE BEING EATEN. IN LATIN AMERICA THE FRUIT IS USED MUCH AS A POTATO WOULD BE. THIS SNACK HAS A LOVELY SWEET TASTE, WHICH IS BALANCED BY THE HEAT FROM THE CHILLI POWDER AND SAUCE. COOK THE CHIPS JUST BEFORE YOU PLAN TO SERVE THEM.

SERVES FOUR AS AN APPETIZER OR SNACK

INGREDIENTS
2 large plantains
oil, for shallow frying
2.5ml/½ tsp chilli powder
5ml/1 tsp ground cinnamon
hot chilli sauce, to serve

COOK'S TIP
Plantain skins are very dark, almost black, when the fruit is ready to eat. If they are green when you buy them, allow them to ripen at room temperature for a few days before use.

1 Peel the plantains. Cut off and throw away the ends, then slice the fruit into rounds, cutting slightly on the diagonal to give larger, flatter slices.

2 Pour the oil for frying into a small frying pan, to a depth of about 1cm/½in. Heat the oil until it is very hot, watching it closely all the time. Test by carefully adding a slice of plantain; it should float and the oil should immediately bubble up around it.

3 Fry the plantain slices in small batches or the temperature of the oil will drop. When they are golden brown remove from the oil with a slotted spoon and drain on kitchen paper.

4 Mix the chilli powder with the cinnamon. Put the plantain chips on a serving plate, sprinkle them with the chilli and cinnamon mixture and serve immediately, with a small bowl of hot chilli sauce for dipping.

POPCORN WITH LIME AND CHILLI

IF THE ONLY POPCORN YOU'VE HAD CAME OUT OF A CARTON AT THE CINEMA, TRY THIS MEXICAN SPECIALITY. THE LIME JUICE AND CHILLI POWDER ARE INSPIRED ADDITIONS, AND THE SNACK IS QUITE A HEALTHY CHOICE TO SERVE WITH DRINKS.

MAKES ONE LARGE BOWL

INGREDIENTS
   30ml/2 tbsp vegetable oil
   225g/8oz/1¼ cups corn kernels
      for popcorn
   10ml/2 tsp chilli powder
   juice of 2 limes

1 Heat the oil in a large, heavy frying pan until it is very hot. Add the popcorn and immediately cover the pan with a lid and reduce the heat.

2 After a few minutes the corn should start to pop. Resist the temptation to lift the lid to check. Shake the pan occasionally so that all corn will be cooked and browned.

3 When the sound of popping corn has stopped, quickly remove the pan from the heat and allow to cool slightly. Take off the lid and with a spoon lift out and discard any corn kernels that have not popped. The uncooked corn will have fallen to the bottom of the pan and is completely inedible.

4 Add the chilli powder. Shake the pan again and again to make sure that all of the corn is covered with a colourful dusting of chilli.

5 Tip the popcorn into a large bowl and keep warm. Add a squeeze of lime juice immediately before serving.

Meat
Dishes

In Mexico the main meal of the day is eaten at a leisurely pace from about 3pm, and is called
comida. The first dish will be one or two appetizers followed by soup, then a rice or pasta dish, then
sometimes a fish or vegetable dish, after which will come the meat course. The meat course is typically
served with corn tortillas and a salad, and some level of chilli is almost inevitable, whether it is the
nutty flavour of cascabel with creamy pork enchiladas, the distinctively rich and smoky flavour of
chipotle chillies with chicken or the almost liquorice-like pasilla used to flavour a hearty lamb stew.

CHICKEN FAJITAS

THE PERFECT DISH FOR CASUAL ENTERTAINING, FAJITAS ARE FLOUR TORTILLAS WHICH ARE BROUGHT TO THE TABLE FRESHLY COOKED. GUESTS ADD THEIR OWN FILLINGS BEFORE FOLDING THE TORTILLAS AND TUCKING IN.

SERVES SIX

INGREDIENTS
  3 skinless, boneless chicken
    breast portions
  finely grated rind and juice of 2 limes
  30ml/2 tbsp caster (superfine) sugar
  10ml/2 tsp dried oregano
  2.5ml/½ tsp cayenne pepper
  5ml/1 tsp ground cinnamon
  2 onions
  3 (bell) peppers
  45ml/3 tbsp vegetable oil
  guacamole, salsa and sour cream,
    to serve
For the tortillas
  250g/9oz/2¼ cups plain (all-purpose)
    flour, sifted
  1.5ml/¼ tsp baking powder
  pinch of salt
  50g/2oz/¼ cup lard (shortening)
  60ml/4 tbsp warm water

1 Slice the chicken into 2cm/¾in wide strips and place these in a large bowl. Add the lime rind and juice, caster sugar, oregano, cayenne and cinnamon. Mix thoroughly. Set aside to marinate for at least 30 minutes.

COOK'S TIP
Tortilla dough can be very difficult to roll out thinly. If the dough is breaking up, try placing each ball between 2 sheets of clean plastic (this can be cut from a new sandwich bag). Roll out, turning over, still inside the plastic, until the tortilla is the right size.

2 Meanwhile, make the tortillas. Mix the flour, baking powder and salt in a large bowl. Rub in the lard, then add the warm water, a little at a time, to make a stiff dough. Knead this on a lightly floured surface for 10–15 minutes until it is smooth and elastic.

3 Divide the dough into 12 small balls, then roll each ball to a 15cm/6in round. Cover them with plastic or clear film (plastic wrap) to keep them from drying out while you prepare the vegetables.

4 Cut the onions in half and slice them thinly. Cut the peppers in half, remove the cores and seeds, then slice the flesh into 1cm/½in wide strips.

5 Heat a large frying pan or griddle and cook each tortilla in turn for about 1 minute on each side, or until the surface colours and begins to blister. Keep the cooked tortillas warm and pliable by wrapping them in a clean, dry dishtowel.

6 Heat the oil in a large frying pan. Stir-fry the marinated chicken for 5–6 minutes, then add the peppers and onions and cook for 3–4 minutes more, until the chicken strips are cooked through and the vegetables are soft and tender, but still juicy.

7 Spoon the chicken mixture into a serving bowl and take it to the table with the cooked tortillas, guacamole, salsa and sour cream. Keep the tortillas wrapped and warm.

8 To serve, each guest takes a warm tortilla, spreads it with a little salsa, adds a spoonful of guacamole and piles some of the chicken mixture in the centre. The final touch is to add a small spoon of sour cream. The tortilla is then folded over the filling and eaten in the hand.

CHICKEN WITH CHIPOTLE SAUCE

IT IS IMPORTANT TO SEEK OUT CHIPOTLE CHILLIES FOR THIS RECIPE, AS THEY IMPART A WONDERFULLY RICH AND SMOKY FLAVOUR TO THE CHICKEN. THE PURÉE CAN BE MADE AHEAD OF TIME, MAKING THIS A VERY EASY RECIPE FOR ENTERTAINING.

SERVES SIX

INGREDIENTS
    6 chipotle chillies
    200ml/7fl oz/scant 1 cup hot water
    chicken stock (see method)
    3 onions
    6 boneless chicken breast portions
    45ml/3 tbsp vegetable oil
    salt and ground black pepper
    fresh oregano to garnish

1 Put the dried chillies in a bowl and pour over the hot water. Leave to stand for about 30 minutes until very soft. Drain, reserving the soaking water in a measuring jug (cup). Cut off the stalk from each chilli, then slit them lengthwise and scrape out the seeds with a small sharp knife.

2 Preheat the oven to 180°C/350°F/Gas 4. Chop the flesh of the chillies coarsely and put it in a food processor or blender. Add enough chicken stock to the soaking water to make it up to 400ml/14fl oz/1⅔ cups. Pour it into the processor or blender and process at maximum power until smooth.

3 Peel the onions. Using a sharp knife, cut them in half, then slice them thinly. Separate the slices.

4 Remove the skin from the chicken breast portions and trim off any stray pieces of fat or membrane.

5 Heat the oil in a large frying pan, add the onions and cook over a low to moderate heat for about 5 minutes, or until they have softened but not coloured, stirring occasionally.

6 Using a slotted spoon, transfer the onion slices to a casserole that is large enough to hold all the chicken breast portions in a single layer. Sprinkle the onion slices with a little salt and ground black pepper.

COOK'S TIP
If you are a lover of chipotle chillies, you may wish to use more than 6.

7 Arrange the chicken breast portions on top of the onion slices. Sprinkle with a little salt and several grindings of black pepper.

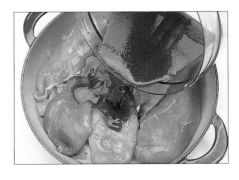

8 Pour the chipotle purée over the chicken, making sure that each piece is evenly coated.

9 Place the casserole in the preheated oven and bake for 45 minutes–1 hour or until the chicken is cooked through, but is still moist and tender. Garnish with fresh oregano and serve with boiled white rice, and *Frijoles de Olla*.

TURKEY MOLE

A MOLE IS A RICH STEW, TRADITIONALLY SERVED ON A FESTIVE OCCASION. THE WORD COMES FROM THE AZTEC "MOLLI", MEANING A CHILLI-FLAVOURED SAUCE. THERE ARE MANY DIFFERENT TYPES, INCLUDING THE FAMOUS MOLE POBLANO DE GUAJALOTE. TOASTED NUTS, FRUIT AND CHOCOLATE ARE AMONG THE CLASSIC INGREDIENTS; THIS VERSION INCLUDES COCOA POWDER.

SERVES FOUR

INGREDIENTS

1 ancho chilli, seeded
1 guajillo chilli, seeded
115g/4oz/¾ cup sesame seeds
50g/2oz/½ cup blanched almonds
50g/2oz/½ cup shelled unsalted
   peanuts, skinned
1 small onion
2 garlic cloves
50g/2oz/¼ cup lard (shortening) or
   60ml/4 tbsp vegetable oil
50g/2oz/⅓ cup canned tomatoes in
   tomato juice
1 ripe plantain
50g/2oz/⅓ cup raisins
75g/3oz/½ cup ready-to-eat
   prunes, stoned (pitted)
5ml/1 tsp dried oregano
2.5ml/½ tsp ground cloves
2.5ml/½ tsp crushed allspice berries
5ml/1 tsp ground cinnamon
25g/1oz/¼ cup cocoa powder
   (unsweetened)
4 turkey breast steaks
fresh oregano, to garnish (optional)

1 Soak both types of dried chilli in a bowl of hot water for 30 minutes, then lift them out and chop them coarsely. Reserve 250ml/8fl oz/1 cup of the soaking liquid.

COOK'S TIP
It is important to use good quality cocoa powder, which is unsweetened.

2 Spread out the sesame seeds in a heavy frying pan. Toast them over a moderate heat, shaking the pan lightly so that they turn golden all over. Do not let them burn, or the sauce will taste bitter. Set aside 45ml/3 tbsp of the toasted seeds for the garnish and tip the rest into a bowl. Toast the almonds and peanuts in the same way and add them to the bowl.

3 Chop the onion and garlic finely. Heat half the lard or oil in a frying pan, cook the chopped onion and garlic for 2–3 minutes, then add the chillies and tomatoes. Cook gently for 10 minutes.

4 Peel the plantain and slice it into short diagonal slices. Add it to the onion mixture with the raisins, prunes, dried oregano, spices and cocoa. Stir in the 250ml/8fl oz/1 cup of the reserved water in which the chillies were soaked. Bring to the boil, stirring, then add the toasted sesame seeds, almonds and peanuts. Cook for 10 minutes, stirring frequently, then remove from the heat and leave to cool slightly.

5 Blend the sauce in batches in a food processor or blender until smooth. The sauce should be fairly thick, but a little water may be added if necessary.

6 Heat the remaining lard or oil in a flameproof casserole. Add the turkey and brown over a moderate heat.

7 Pour the sauce over the steaks and cover the casserole with foil and a tight-fitting lid. Cook over a gentle heat for 20–25 minutes or until the turkey is cooked, and the sauce has thickened. Sprinkle with sesame seeds and chopped oregano, and serve with a rice dish and warm tortillas.

CHICKEN AND TOMATILLO CHIMICHANGAS

THESE FRIED BURRITOS ARE A COMMON SIGHT ON STREET STALLS AND IN CAFÉS ALONG THE MEXICAN BORDER WITH TEXAS, BUT ARE NOT SO WELL KNOWN FURTHER SOUTH.

SERVES FOUR

INGREDIENTS
 2 skinless, boneless chicken
   breast portions
 1 chipotle chilli, seeded
 15ml/1 tbsp vegetable oil
 2 onions, finely chopped
 4 garlic cloves, crushed
 2.5ml/½ tsp ground cumin
 2.5ml/½ tsp ground coriander
 2.5ml/½ tsp ground cinnamon
 2.5ml/½ tsp ground cloves
 300g/11oz/scant 2 cups drained
   canned tomatillos
 400g/14oz/2⅓ cups cooked
   pinto beans
 8 x 20–25cm/8–10in fresh wheat
   flour tortillas
 oil, for frying
 salt and ground black pepper

1 Put the chicken in a large pan, pour over water to cover and add the chilli. Bring to the boil, lower the heat and simmer for 10 minutes or until the chicken is cooked through. Remove the chilli and chop it finely. Lift the chicken breast portions out of the pan and put them on a plate. Leave to cool slightly, then shred with 2 forks.

2 Heat the oil in a frying pan. Cook the onions until translucent, then add the garlic and ground spices and cook for 3 minutes more. Add the tomatillos and pinto beans. Cook over a moderate heat for 5 minutes, stirring constantly to break up the tomatillos and some of the beans. Simmer gently for 5 minutes more. Add the chicken and seasoning.

3 Wrap the tortillas in foil and place them on a plate. Stand the plate over boiling water for about 5 minutes until they become pliable. Alternatively, wrap them in microwave-safe film and heat them in a microwave on full power for 1 minute.

4 Spoon one-eighth of the bean filling into the centre of a tortilla, fold in both sides, then fold the bottom up and the top down to form a parcel. Secure with a cocktail stick or toothpick.

5 Heat the oil in a large frying pan and fry the chimichangas in batches until crisp, turning once. Remove them from the oil with a slotted spoon and drain on kitchen paper. Serve hot.

COOK'S TIP
The word "pinto" means speckled, which aptly describes these attractive dried beans. If you prepare them yourself, they will need to be soaked overnight in water, then cooked in unsalted boiling water for 1–1¼ hours until tender.

BEEF ENCHILADAS <u>WITH</u> RED SAUCE

ENCHILADAS ARE USUALLY MADE WITH CORN TORTILLAS, ALTHOUGH IN PARTS OF NORTHERN MEXICO FLOUR TORTILLAS ARE SOMETIMES USED.

SERVES THREE TO FOUR

INGREDIENTS

500g/1¼lb rump (round) steak, cut into 5cm/2in cubes
2 ancho chillies, seeded
2 pasilla chillies, seeded
2 garlic cloves, crushed
10ml/2 tsp dried oregano
2.5ml/½ tsp ground cumin
30ml/2 tbsp vegetable oil
7 fresh corn tortillas
shredded onion and flat leaf parsley to garnish
Mango Salsa, to serve

1 Put the steak in a deep frying pan and cover with water. Bring to the boil, then lower the heat and simmer for 1–1½ hours, or until very tender.

2 Meanwhile, put the dried chillies in a bowl and pour over the hot water. Leave to soak for 30 minutes, then tip the contents of the bowl into a blender and process to a smooth paste.

3 Drain the steak and let it cool, reserving 250ml/8fl oz/1 cup of the cooking liquid. Meanwhile, cook the garlic, oregano and cumin in the oil for 2 minutes.

4 Stir in the chilli paste and the reserved cooking liquid from the beef. Tear 1 of the tortillas into small pieces and add it to the mixture. Bring to the boil, then lower the heat. Simmer for 10 minutes, stirring occasionally, until the sauce has thickened. Shred the steak, using 2 forks, and stir it into the sauce, heat through for a few minutes.

5 Spoon some of the meat mixture on to each tortilla and roll it up to make an enchilada. Keep the enchiladas in a warmed dish until you have rolled them all. Garnish with shreds of onion and fresh flat leaf parsley and then serve immediately with the Mango Salsa.

VARIATION
For a richer version place the rolled enchiladas side by side in a gratin dish. Pour over 300ml/½ pint/1¼ cups sour cream and 75g/3oz/¾ cup grated Cheddar cheese. Place under a preheated grill (broiler) for 5 minutes or until the cheese melts and the sauce begins to bubble. Serve immediately.

STUFFED BUTTERFLY OF BEEF WITH CHEESE AND CHILLI SAUCE

THIS RECIPE HAD ITS ORIGINS IN NORTHERN MEXICO OR IN NEW MEXICO, WHICH IS BEEF COUNTRY. IT IS A GOOD WAY TO COOK STEAKS, EITHER UNDER THE GRILL OR ON THE BARBECUE.

SERVES FOUR

INGREDIENTS
  4 fresh serrano chillies
  115g/4oz/½ cup full-fat soft cheese
  30ml/2 tbsp reposada tequila
  30ml/2 tbsp oil
  1 onion
  2 garlic cloves
  5ml/1 tsp dried oregano
  2.5ml/½ tsp salt
  2.5ml/½ tsp ground black pepper
  175g/6oz/1½ cups grated medium
    Cheddar cheese
  4 fillet steaks, at least 2.5cm/
    1in thick

1 Dry roast the chillies in a griddle pan over a moderate heat, turning them frequently until the skins are blistered but not burnt. Put them in a strong plastic bag and tie the top to keep the steam in. Set aside for 20 minutes.

2 Remove the chillies from the bag, slit them and scrape out the seeds with a sharp knife. Cut the flesh into long narrow strips, then cut each strip into several shorter strips.

3 Put the full-fat soft cheese in a small heavy pan and stir over a low heat until it has melted. Add the chilli strips and the tequila and stir to make a smooth sauce. Keep the sauce warm over a very low heat.

4 Heat the oil in a frying pan and cook the onion, garlic and oregano for about 5 minutes over a moderate heat, stirring frequently until the onion has browned. Season with the salt and pepper.

5 Remove the pan from the heat and stir in the grated cheese so that it melts into the onion mixture.

6 Cut each steak almost but not quite in half across its width, so that it can be opened out, butterfly-fashion. Preheat the grill (broiler) to its highest setting.

7 Spoon a quarter of the cheese and onion filling on to 1 side of each steak and close the other side over it. Place the steaks in a grill pan and grill (broil) for 3–5 minutes on each side, depending on how you like your steak. Serve on heated plates with the vegetables of your choice, and with the cheese and chilli sauce poured over.

COOK'S TIP
One of the easiest ways of testing whether a steak is cooked is by touch. A steak that is very rare or "blue" will feel soft to the touch; the meat will be relaxed. A rare steak will feel like a sponge, and will spring back when lightly pressed. A medium-rare steak offers more resistance, while a well-cooked steak will feel very firm.

ENCHILADAS <u>WITH</u> PORK <u>AND</u> GREEN SAUCE

THE GREEN TOMATILLO SAUCE PROVIDES A TART CONTRAST TO THE PORK FILLING IN THIS POPULAR DISH. CASCABELS ARE DRIED CHILLIES WHICH RATTLE WHEN SHAKEN.

SERVES THREE TO FOUR

INGREDIENTS

500g/1¼lb pork shoulder, diced
1 cascabel chilli
30ml/2 tbsp oil
2 garlic cloves, crushed
1 onion, finely chopped
300g/11oz/scant 2 cups drained
  canned tomatillos
6 fresh corn tortillas
75g/3oz/¾ cup grated Monterey Jack
  or mild Cheddar cheese

1 Put the diced pork in a pan and pour over water to cover. Bring to the boil, lower the heat and simmer for 40 minutes.

2 Meanwhile, soak the dried chilli in hot water for 30 minutes until softened. Drain, remove the stalk, then slit the chilli and scrape out the seeds.

3 Drain the pork and let it cool slightly, then shred it, using 2 forks. Put the pork in a bowl and set it aside.

4 Heat the oil in a frying pan and fry the garlic and onion for 3–4 minutes until translucent. Chop and add the chilli with the tomatillos. Cook, stirring constantly, until the tomatillos start to break up. Lower the heat and simmer the sauce for 10 minutes more. Cool slightly, then purée in a blender.

5 Preheat the oven to 180°C/350°F/ Gas 4. Soften the tortillas by wrapping them in foil and steaming on a plate over boiling water for a few minutes until they are pliable. Alternatively, wrap them in microwave-safe film and heat in a microwave on full power for about 30 seconds.

6 Spoon one-sixth of the shredded pork on to the centre of a tortilla and roll it up to make an enchilada. Place it in a shallow ovenproof dish which is large enough to hold all the enchiladas in a single layer. Fill and roll the remaining tortillas and add them to the dish.

7 Pour the sauce over the enchiladas to cover completely. Sprinkle evenly with cheese. Bake for 25–30 minutes or until the cheese bubbles. Serve immediately. A fresh tomato salad makes a good accompaniment for this dish.

PORK IN GREEN SAUCE WITH CACTUS

CHILE VERDE IS A CLASSIC SAUCE. THE INCLUSION OF CACTUS PIECES — A POPULAR INGREDIENT IN MEXICAN COOKING — GIVES THIS DISH AN INTRIGUING FLAVOUR WHICH WILL DOUBTLESS PROVE A GOOD TALKING POINT AT THE DINNER TABLE.

SERVES FOUR

INGREDIENTS

   30ml/2 tbsp vegetable oil
   500g/1¼lb pork shoulder, cut in
    2.5cm/1in cubes
   1 onion, finely chopped
   2 garlic cloves, crushed
   5ml/1 tsp dried oregano
   3 fresh jalapeño chillies, seeded
    and chopped
   300g/11oz/scant 2 cups drained
    canned tomatillos
   150ml/¼ pint/⅔ cup vegetable stock
   300g/11oz jar *nopalitos*, drained
   salt and ground black pepper
   warm fresh corn tortillas, to serve

COOK'S TIP

Nopalitos are cactus paddles which have been cut into strips and pickled in vinegar or packed in brine. Look for them in speciality food stores.

1 Heat the oil in a large pan. Add the pork cubes and cook over a high heat, turning several times until browned all over. Add the onion and garlic and cook gently until soft, then stir in the oregano and chopped jalapeño chillies. Cook for 2 minutes more.

2 Tip the canned tomatillos into a blender, add the stock and process until smooth. Add to the pork mixture, cover and cook for 30 minutes.

3 Meanwhile, soak the *nopalitos* in cold water for 10 minutes. Drain, then add to the pork and continue cooking for about 10 minutes or until the pork is cooked through and tender.

4 Season the mixture with salt and plenty of ground black pepper. Serve with warm corn tortillas.

TORTILLA PIE WITH CHORIZO

THIS IS A POPULAR MEXICAN BREAKFAST DISH, KNOWN AS CHILAQUILES. THE FRIED TORTILLA STRIPS STAY CRISP IN THE TOMATILLO, CREAM AND CHEESE SAUCE.

SERVES SIX

INGREDIENTS
   25g/1oz/2 tbsp lard (shortening) or
      30ml/2 tbsp vegetable oil
   500g/1¼lb minced (ground) pork
   3 garlic cloves, crushed
   10ml/2 tsp dried oregano
   5ml/1 tsp ground cinnamon
   2.5ml/½ tsp ground cloves
   2.5ml/½ tsp ground black pepper
   30ml/2 tbsp dry sherry
   5ml/1 tsp caster (superfine) sugar
   5ml/1 tsp salt
   12 corn tortillas, freshly made or a
      few days old
   oil, for frying
   350g/12oz/3 cups grated Monterey
      Jack or mild Cheddar cheese
   300ml/½ pint/1¼ cups crème fraîche
For the tomatillo sauce
   300g/11oz/scant 2 cups drained
      canned tomatillos
   60ml/4 tbsp stock or water
   2 fresh serrano chillies, seeded and
      coarsely chopped
   2 garlic cloves
   bunch of fresh coriander (cilantro)
   120ml/4fl oz/½ cup sour cream

1 Preheat the oven to 180°C/350°F/ Gas 4. Heat the lard or oil in a large pan. Add the minced pork and crushed garlic. Stir over a moderate heat until the meat has browned, then stir in the oregano, cinnamon, cloves and pepper. Cook for 3–4 minutes more, stirring constantly, then add the sherry, sugar and salt. Stir for 3–4 minutes until all the flavours are blended, then remove the pan from the heat.

2 Cut the tortillas into 2cm/¾in strips. Pour oil into a frying pan to a depth of 2cm/¾in and heat to 190°C/375°F. Fry the tortilla strips in batches until crisp and golden brown all over.

3 Spread half the minced pork mixture in an ovenproof dish. Top with half the tortilla strips and grated cheese, then add spoons of crème fraîche. Repeat the layers. Bake for 20–25 minutes, or until bubbling.

4 To make the sauce, put all the ingredients except the sour cream in a food processor or blender. Reserve a little coriander. Process until smooth. Scrape into a pan, bring to the boil, then lower the heat and simmer for 5 minutes. Chop the reserved coriander.

5 Stir the sour cream into the sauce, with salt and pepper to taste. Pour the mixture over the tortilla pie and serve immediately, sprinkled with coriander.

TOSTADAS WITH SHREDDED PORK AND SPICES

CRISP FRIED TORTILLAS TOPPED WITH REFRIED BEANS AND SPICED SHREDDED PORK MAKE A DELECTABLE TREAT AND ARE OFTEN SOLD FROM STALLS IN MEXICAN CITY STREETS.

SERVES SIX

INGREDIENTS
 6 corn tortillas, freshly made or a few days old
 oil, for frying
For the topping
 500g/1¼lb pork shoulder, cut into 2.5cm/1in cubes
 2.5ml/½ tsp salt
 15ml/1 tbsp oil
 1 small onion, halved and sliced
 1 garlic clove, crushed
 1 pasilla chilli, seeded and ground
 5ml/1 tsp ground cinnamon
 2.5ml/½ tsp ground cloves
 175g/6oz/1 cup Refried Beans
 90ml/6 tbsp sour cream
 2 tomatoes, seeded and diced
 115g/4oz feta cheese, crumbled
 fresh oregano sprigs, to garnish

COOK'S TIP
In Mexico, the local fresh goat's or cow's cheese – *queso fresco* – would be used; feta is the nearest equivalent.

1 Make the topping. Place the pork cubes in a pan, pour over water to cover and bring to the boil. Lower the heat, cover and simmer for 40 minutes. Drain, discarding the cooking liquid. Shred the pork, using 2 forks. Put it in a bowl and season with the salt.

2 Heat the oil in a large frying pan. Add the onion, garlic, chilli and spices. Stir over the heat for 2–3 minutes, then add the shredded meat and cook until the meat is thoroughly heated and has absorbed the flavourings. Heat the refried beans in a separate, small pan.

3 Meanwhile, cook the tortillas. Pour oil into a large frying pan to a depth of 2cm/¾in. Heat the oil and fry one tortilla at a time, pressing down with a spatula or a pair of tongs to keep it flat. As soon as a tortilla is crisp, lift it out and drain it on kitchen paper.

4 Place each tortilla on a plate. Top with refried beans. Add a little of the meat mixture, then spoon 15ml/1 tbsp of the sour cream over each. Divide the chopped tomato among the tostadas and top with the crumbled feta. Serve immediately, garnished with oregano.

TAMALES FILLED WITH SPICED PORK

These tamales are among the most ancient of Mexican foods. At one time the neat little corn husk parcels filled with plain, savoury or sweet masa dough were cooked in the ashes of a wood fire. Today they are more likely to be steamed, but the thrill of unwrapping them remains the same.

SERVES SIX

INGREDIENTS

- 500g/1¼lb lean pork, cut into 5cm/2in cubes
- 750ml/1¼ pints/3 cups chicken stock
- 600g/1lb 6oz/4½ cups *masa harina*
- 450g/1lb/2 cups lard (shortening)
- 30ml/2 tbsp salt
- 12 large or 24 small dried corn husks
- 2 ancho chillies, seeded
- 15ml/1 tbsp vegetable oil
- ½ onion, finely chopped
- 2–3 garlic cloves, crushed
- 2.5ml/½ tsp allspice berries
- 2 dried bay leaves
- 2.5ml/½ tsp ground cumin
- lime wedges, to serve (optional)

1 Put the pork cubes in a large pan. Pour over water to cover. Bring to the boil, lower the heat and simmer for 40 minutes.

2 Meanwhile, heat the chicken stock in a separate pan. Put the *masa harina* in a large bowl and add the hot stock, a little at a time, to make a stiff dough.

3 Put the lard in another bowl and beat with an electric whisk until light and fluffy, as when beating butter for a cake. Test by dropping a small amount of the whipped lard into a cup of water. If it floats, it is ready for use.

4 Continue to beat the lard, gradually adding the *masa* dough. When all of it has been added and the mixture is light and spreadable, beat in the salt. Cover closely with clear film (plastic wrap) to prevent the mixture from drying out.

5 Put the corn husks in a bowl and pour over boiling water to cover. Leave to soak for 30 minutes. Soak the seeded chillies in a separate bowl of hot water for the same time. Drain the pork, reserving 105ml/7 tbsp of the cooking liquid, and chop the meat finely.

6 Heat the oil in a large pan and cook the onion and garlic over a moderate heat for 2–3 minutes. Drain the chillies, chop them finely and add them to the pan. Put the allspice berries and bay leaves in a mortar, grind them with a pestle, then work in the ground cumin. Add to the onion mixture and stir well. Cook for 2–3 minutes more. Add the chopped pork and reserved cooking liquid and continue cooking over a moderate heat until all the liquid has evaporated. Leave to cool slightly.

7 Drain the corn husks and pat them dry in a clean dishtowel. Place a large corn husk (or overlap 2 smaller ones) on a board. Spoon about one-twelfth of the *masa* mixture on to the centre of the husk wrapping and spread it almost to the sides.

8 Place a spoonful of the meat mixture on top of the *masa*. Fold the 2 long sides of the corn husk over the filling, then bring up each of the 2 shorter sides in turn, to make a neat parcel. Slide 1 of the 2 short sides inside the other, if possible, to prevent the parcel from unravelling, or tie with string or strips of the corn husk.

9 Place the *tamales* in a steamer basket over a pan of steadily simmering water and steam for 1 hour, adding more water as needed. To test if the *tamales* are ready, unwrap one. The filling should peel away from the husk cleanly. Pile the *tamales* on a plate, leave to stand for 10 minutes, then serve with lime wedges, if you like. Guests unwrap their own *tamales* at the table.

CARNITAS

Succulent little pieces of meat, usually pork, carnitas, literally "little meats", can be eaten as part of a main dish or used to fill tacos or burritos. They are also served with salsa as snacks or antojitos *(nibbles).*

SERVES EIGHT AS AN APPETIZER,
SIX AS A MAIN COURSE

INGREDIENTS
  2 dried bay leaves
  10ml/2 tsp dried thyme
  5ml/1 tsp dried marjoram
  1.5kg/3–3½lb mixed boneless pork
    (loin and leg)
  2.5ml/½ tsp salt
  200g/7oz/scant 1 cup lard
    (shortening)
  1 orange, cut into 8 wedges
  3 garlic cloves
  1 small onion, thickly sliced
  warm wheat flour tortillas, to serve
For the salsa
  bunch of fresh coriander (cilantro)
  1 white onion
  8–10 pickled jalapeño chilli slices
  45ml/3 tbsp fresh orange juice

1 Crumble the bay leaves into a mortar. Add the dried thyme and dried marjoram and grind the mixture with a pestle to a fine powder.

COOK'S TIP
If the *carnitas* are to be served in tacos or burritos, shred or chop them. Make the chunks about half the given size if serving them as *antojitos*. Reduce the cooking time accordingly.

2 Cut the pork into 5cm/2in cubes and place it in a non-metallic bowl. Add the herbs and salt. Using your fingers, rub the herb mixture into the meat. Cover and marinate for at least 2 hours, preferably overnight.

3 To make the salsa, remove the stems from the coriander and chop the leaves coarsely. Cut the onion in half, then slice each half thinly. Finely chop the jalapeño chilli slices.

4 Mix all the salsa ingredients in a bowl, pour over the fresh orange juice and toss gently to mix. Cover and chill in the refrigerator until required.

5 Heat the lard in a flameproof casserole. Add the pork mixture, with the orange, garlic cloves and onion. Brown the pork cubes on all sides.

6 Using a slotted spoon, lift out the onion and garlic and discard. Cover the casserole and continue to cook over a low heat for about 1½ hours.

7 Remove the lid and lift out and discard the orange wedges. Continue to cook the mixture, uncovered, until all the meat juices have evaporated and the pork cubes are crisp on the outside and tender and moist inside. Serve with warm tortillas and the salsa.

LAMB STEW WITH CHILLI SAUCE

THE CHILLIES IN THIS STEW ADD DEPTH AND RICHNESS TO THE SAUCE, WHILE THE POTATO SLICES ENSURE THAT IT IS SUBSTANTIAL ENOUGH TO SERVE ON ITS OWN.

SERVES SIX

INGREDIENTS
   6 guajillo chillies, seeded
   2 pasilla chillies, seeded
   250ml/8fl oz/1 cup hot water
   3 garlic cloves, peeled
   5ml/1 tsp ground cinnamon
   2.5ml/½ tsp ground cloves
   2.5ml/½ tsp ground black pepper
   15ml/1 tbsp vegetable oil
   1kg/2¼lb lean boneless lamb
     shoulder, cut into 2cm/¾in cubes
   400g/14oz potatoes, scrubbed and
     cut into 1cm/½in thick slices
   salt
   strips of red (bell) pepper and fresh
     oregano to garnish

COOK'S TIP
When frying the lamb, don't be tempted to cook too many cubes at one time, as the meat will steam rather than fry.

1 Snap or tear the dried chillies into large pieces, put them in a bowl and pour over the hot water. Leave to soak for 30 minutes, then tip the contents of the bowl into a food processor or blender. Add the garlic and spices. Process until smooth.

2 Heat the oil in a large pan. Add the lamb cubes, in batches, and stir-fry over a high heat until the cubes are browned on all sides.

3 Return all the lamb cubes to the pan, spread them out, then cover them with a layer of potato slices. Add salt to taste. Put a lid on the pan and cook over a medium heat for 10 minutes.

4 Pour over the chilli mixture and mix well. Replace the lid and simmer over a low heat for about 1 hour or until the meat and the potatoes are tender. Serve with a rice dish, and garnish with strips of red pepper and fresh oregano.

ALBONDIGAS

DON'T BE DAUNTED BY THE LENGTH OF THE INGREDIENT LIST. THESE MEATBALLS ARE ABSOLUTELY DELICIOUS AND THE CHIPOTLE CHILLI GIVES THE SAUCE A DISTINCTIVE, SLIGHTLY SMOKY FLAVOUR.

SERVES FOUR

INGREDIENTS
225g/8oz minced (ground) pork
225g/8oz lean minced (ground) beef
1 onion, finely chopped
50g/2oz/1 cup fresh white
  breadcrumbs
5ml/1 tsp dried oregano
2.5ml/½ tsp ground cumin
2.5ml/½ tsp salt
2.5ml/½ tsp ground black pepper
1 egg, beaten
oil, for frying
fresh oregano sprigs, to garnish
For the sauce
1 chipotle chilli, seeded
15ml/1 tbsp vegetable oil
1 onion, finely chopped
2 garlic cloves, crushed
175ml/6fl oz/¾ cup beef stock
400g/14oz can chopped tomatoes in
  tomato juice
105ml/7 tbsp passata (bottled
  strained tomatoes)

1 Put the pork and beef in a bowl. Add the onion, breadcrumbs, oregano, cumin, salt and pepper. Mix with clean hands until well combined.

2 Stir in the egg, mix well, then roll into 4cm/1½in balls. Put these on a baking sheet and chill while you prepare the sauce.

3 Soak the dried chilli in hot water to cover for 15 minutes. Heat the oil in a pan and cook the onion and garlic for 3–4 minutes until softened.

4 Drain the chilli, reserving the soaking water, then chop it and add it to the onion mixture. Cook for 1 minute, then stir in the beef stock, tomatoes, passata and soaking water, with salt and pepper to taste. Bring to the boil, lower the heat and simmer, stirring occasionally, while you cook the meatballs.

5 Heat the oil for frying in a frying pan and fry the meatballs in batches for about 5 minutes, turning them occasionally, until browned.

6 Drain off the oil and transfer all the meatballs to a shallow casserole. Pour over the sauce and simmer for 10 minutes, stirring gently from time to time so that the meatballs are coated but do not disintegrate. Garnish with the oregano and serve. Plain white rice makes a good accompaniment.

COOK'S TIP
Dampen your hands before shaping the meatballs and the mixture will be less likely to stick.

Fish
and Shellfish

The coastal regions of Mexico are well stocked with fish, especially bass, tuna and swordfish, and there are many traditional Mexican recipes that use locally caught shellfish. Salt cod, which was once the only way inland Mexicans could have access to fish, is now a much-loved delicacy and is used in some of Mexico's oldest recipes. Fresh fish needs to be cooked gently so that the delicate flavours are not lost, and chillies need to be used with care. Small amounts of green chillies and pickled jalapeno chillies are often used with simply fried white fish, but meatier fish can take more robust chilli infusions, such as fresh serrano chillies with swordfish steaks or hot chilli sauce with scallops.

ESCABECHE

A CLASSIC DISH THAT THE MEXICANS INHERITED FROM THE SPANISH, ESCABECHE IS OFTEN CONFUSED WITH CEVICHE, WHICH CONSISTS OF MARINATED RAW FISH. IN ESCABECHE, THE RAW FISH IS INITIALLY MARINATED IN LIME JUICE, BUT IS THEN COOKED BEFORE BEING PICKLED.

SERVES FOUR

INGREDIENTS
   900g/2lb whole fish fillets
   juice of 2 limes
   300ml/½ pint/1¼ cups olive oil
   6 peppercorns
   3 garlic cloves, sliced
   2.5ml/½ tsp ground cumin
   2.5ml/½ tsp dried oregano
   2 bay leaves
   50g/2oz/⅓ cup pickled jalapeño chilli
      slices, chopped
   1 onion, thinly sliced
   250ml/8fl oz/1 cup white wine vinegar
   150g/5oz/1¼ cups green olives
      stuffed with pimiento, to garnish

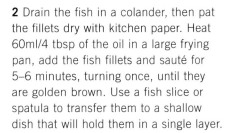

1 Place the fish fillets in a single layer in a shallow non-metallic dish. Pour the lime juice over, turn the fillets over once to ensure that they are completely coated, then cover the dish and leave to marinate for 15 minutes.

2 Drain the fish in a colander, then pat the fillets dry with kitchen paper. Heat 60ml/4 tbsp of the oil in a large frying pan, add the fish fillets and sauté for 5–6 minutes, turning once, until they are golden brown. Use a fish slice or spatula to transfer them to a shallow dish that will hold them in a single layer.

3 Heat 30ml/2 tbsp of the remaining oil in a frying pan. Add the peppercorns, garlic, ground cumin, oregano, bay leaves and jalapeños, and cook over a low heat for 2 minutes, then increase the heat, add the onion slices and vinegar and bring to the boil. Lower the heat and simmer for 4 minutes.

4 Remove the pan from the heat and carefully add the remaining oil. Stir well, then pour the mixture over the fish. Leave to cool, then cover the dish and marinate for 24 hours in the refrigerator.

5 When you are ready to serve, drain off the liquid and garnish the pickled fish with the stuffed olives. Salad leaves would make a good accompaniment.

COOK'S TIP
Use the largest frying pan you have when cooking the fish. If your pan is too small, it may be necessary to cook them in batches. Do not overcrowd the pan as they will cook unevenly.

VERACRUZ-STYLE RED SNAPPER

THIS IS A CLASSIC MEXICAN DISH WHICH BORROWS BAY LEAVES AND OLIVES FROM SPAIN TO GO WITH THE NATIVE CHILLIES. FOR EXTRA HEAT, SERVE SPRINKLED WITH STRIPS OF GREEN CHILLI.

SERVES FOUR

INGREDIENTS
    4 whole red snapper, cleaned
    juice of 2 limes
    4 garlic cloves, crushed
    5ml/1 tsp dried oregano
    2.5ml/½ tsp salt
    drained bottled capers, to garnish
    lime wedges, to serve (optional)
For the sauce
    120ml/4fl oz/½ cup olive oil
    2 bay leaves
    2 garlic cloves, sliced
    4 fresh jalapeño chillies, seeded and
      cut in strips
    1 onion, thinly sliced
    8 fresh tomatoes
    75g/3oz/½ cup pickled jalapeño
      chilli slices
    15ml/1 tbsp soft dark brown sugar
    2.5ml/½ tsp ground cloves
    2.5ml/½ tsp ground cinnamon
    150g/5oz/1¼ cups green olives
      stuffed with pimiento

4 Add the onion slices to the olive oil in the pan and cook for 3–4 minutes more, until all the onion is softened and translucent.

5 Cut a cross in the base of each tomato. Place them in a heatproof bowl and pour over boiling water to cover. After 3 minutes, lift the tomatoes out on a slotted spoon and plunge them into a bowl of cold water. Drain. The skins will have begun to peel back from the crosses.

6 Peel the tomatoes completely, then cut them in half and squeeze out the seeds. Chop the flesh finely and add it to the onion mixture. Cook for 3–4 minutes, until the tomato is starting to soften.

7 Add the pickled jalapeños, brown sugar, ground cloves and cinnamon to the sauce. Cook for 10 minutes, stirring frequently, then stir the olives into the sauce and pour a little over each fish. Garnish with the capers and serve with lime wedges, if you like. A rice dish would make a good accompaniment.

1 Preheat the oven to 180°C/350°F/Gas 4. Rinse the fish inside and out, then pat dry with kitchen paper. Place in roasting pans in a single layer.

2 Mix the lime juice, garlic, oregano and salt in a small bowl. Pour the mixture over the fish. Bake for about 30 minutes, or until the flesh flakes easily when tested with the tip of a sharp knife.

3 Meanwhile, make the sauce. Heat the olive oil in a pan, add the bay leaves, garlic and chilli strips and cook over a low heat for 3–4 minutes.

SALT COD <u>FOR</u> CHRISTMAS EVE

THIS MEXICAN DISH IS MILDER THAN THE SIMILAR SPANISH DISH, BACALAO A LA VIZCAÍNA. IT IS EATEN ON CHRISTMAS EVE THROUGHOUT MEXICO.

SERVES SIX

INGREDIENTS

450g/1lb dried salt cod
105ml/7 tbsp extra virgin olive oil
1 onion, halved and thinly sliced
4 garlic cloves, crushed
2 x 400g/14oz cans chopped
  tomatoes in tomato juice
75g/3oz/¾ cup flaked
  (sliced) almonds
75g/3oz/½ cup pickled jalapeño
  chilli slices
115g/4oz/1 cup green olives stuffed
  with pimiento
bunch of fresh parsley, chopped
salt and ground black pepper
fresh flat leaf parsley, to garnish
crusty bread, to serve

1 Put the cod in a large bowl and pour over enough cold water to cover. Soak for 24 hours, changing the water at least five times during this period.

2 Drain the cod and remove the skin using a large sharp knife. Shred the flesh finely using 2 forks, and put it into a bowl. Set it aside.

3 Heat half the oil in a large frying pan. Add the onion slices and cook over a moderate heat until the onion has softened and is translucent.

4 Remove the onion from the pan and set aside. Make sure you transfer the oil with the onion as it is an important flavouring in this dish and must not be discarded. Add the remaining olive oil to the same pan. When the oil is hot but not smoking, add the crushed garlic and cook gently for 2 minutes.

5 Add the canned tomatoes and their juice to the pan with the garlic. Cook over a medium-high heat for about 20 minutes, stirring occasionally, until the mixture has reduced and thickened.

COOK'S TIPS
• Salt cod is available in specialist fishmongers, Spanish delicatessens and West Indian stores.
• Any leftovers can be used to fill burritos or empanadas.

6 Meanwhile, cut the almonds in strips and spread them in a single layer in a large, heavy frying pan. Toast them over a moderate heat for a few minutes, shaking the pan lightly throughout the process so that they turn golden brown all over. Do not let them burn.

7 Add the jalapeño chilli slices and stuffed olives to the toasted almonds.

8 Stir in the shredded fish, mixing it in thoroughly, and cook for 20 minutes more, stirring occasionally, until the mixture is almost dry.

9 Season to taste, add the parsley and cook for a further 2–3 minutes. Garnish with parsley leaves and serve in heated bowls, with crusty bread.

RED SNAPPER BURRITOS

FISH MAKES A GREAT FILLING FOR A TORTILLA, ESPECIALLY WHEN IT IS SUCCULENT RED SNAPPER MIXED WITH RICE, CHILLI AND TOMATOES.

SERVES FOUR

INGREDIENTS
    3 red snapper fillets
    90g/3½ oz/½ cup long grain white rice
    30ml/2 tbsp vegetable oil
    1 small onion, finely chopped
    5ml/1 tsp ground achiote seed
        (annatto powder)
    1 pasilla or similar dried chilli,
        seeded and ground
    75g/3oz/¾ cup flaked
        (sliced) almonds
    200g/7oz can chopped tomatoes
    150g/5oz/1¼ cups grated Monterey
        Jack or mild Cheddar cheese
    8 x 20cm/8in wheat flour tortillas
    sliced spring onions (scallions) and
        lime wedges to garnish

1 Preheat the grill (broiler). Grill (broil) the fish on an oiled rack for 5 minutes, turning once. When cool, remove the skin and flake the fish into a bowl.

2 Meanwhile, put the rice in a pan, cover with cold water, cover and bring to the boil. Drain, rinse and drain again.

3 Heat the oil in a pan and cook the onion until soft and translucent. Stir in the ground achiote and the chilli and cook for 5 minutes.

4 Add the rice, stir well, then stir in the fish and almonds. Add the tomatoes, with their juice. Cook over a moderate heat until the juice is absorbed and the rice is tender. Stir in the cheese and remove from the heat. Warm the tortillas.

5 Divide the filling among the tortillas and fold them as shown, to make neat parcels. Place on serving plates and garnish with the sliced spring onions and lime wedges. A green salad makes a good accompaniment.

SEA BASS WITH ORANGE CHILLI SALSA

THE CITRUS SALSA HAS A FRESHNESS WHICH PROVIDES THE PERFECT CONTRAST TO THE WONDERFUL FLAVOUR OF FRESH SEA BASS.

SERVES FOUR

INGREDIENTS
   4 sea bass fillets
   salt and ground black pepper
   fresh coriander (cilantro), to garnish
For the salsa
   2 fresh green chillies
   2 oranges or pink grapefruit
   1 small onion

1 Make the salsa. Roast the chillies in a dry griddle pan until the skins are blistered, being careful not to let the flesh burn. Put them in a strong plastic bag and tie the top to keep the steam in. Set aside for 20 minutes.

COOK'S TIP
If the fish has not been scaled, do this by running the back of a small filleting knife against the grain of the scales. They should come away cleanly. Rinse and pat dry with kitchen paper.

2 Slice the top and bottom off each orange or grapefruit and cut off all the peel and pith. Cut between the membranes and put each segment in a bowl.

3 Remove the chillies from the bag and peel off the skins. Cut off the stalks, then slit the chillies and scrape out the seeds. Chop the flesh finely. Cut the onion in half and slice it thinly. Add the onion and chillies to the orange pieces and mix lightly. Season and chill.

4 Season the fish. Line a steamer with greaseproof (waxed) paper, allowing extra to hang over the sides to enable the fish to be lifted out after cooking. Place the empty steamer over a pan of water and bring to the boil.

5 Place the fish in a single layer in the steamer. Cover with a lid and steam for about 8 minutes or until just cooked. Garnish with fresh coriander and serve with the salsa and a vegetable side dish of your choice.

FRIED SOLE <u>WITH</u> LIME

SIMPLE FISH DISHES LIKE THIS ONE CAPITALIZE ON THE DELICIOUS FLAVOUR OF GOOD FRESH FISH.

SERVES FOUR

INGREDIENTS
  75g/3oz/¾ cup plain (all-
    purpose) flour
  10ml/2 tsp garlic salt
  5ml/1 tsp ground black pepper
  4 sole fillets
  oil, for frying
  juice of 2 limes
  small bunch of fresh parsley,
    chopped, plus extra sprigs,
    to garnish
  fresh salsa, to serve

COOK'S TIP
Make sure the oil is hot enough when
you add the fish, or it will be absorbed
by the fish and the dish will be
too greasy.

1 Mix the flour, garlic salt and pepper together. Spread out the seasoned flour mixture in a shallow dish. Pat the sole fillets dry with kitchen paper, then turn them in the seasoned flour until they are evenly coated.

2 Pour oil into a wide frying pan to a depth of 2.5cm/½in. Heat it until a cube of bread added to the oil rises to the surface and browns in 45–60 seconds.

3 Add the fish, in batches if necessary, and fry for 3–4 minutes. Lift each fillet out and drain it on kitchen paper. Transfer to a heated serving dish.

4 Squeeze the juice of half a lime over each piece of fish and sprinkle with the chopped parsley. Serve immediately, with a fresh salsa to complement the fish. Garnish with parsley sprigs. New potatoes would also go well.

BAKED SALMON <u>WITH A</u> GUAVA SAUCE

GUAVAS HAVE A CREAMY FLESH WITH A SLIGHT CITRUS TANG, WHICH MAKES THEM THE PERFECT FRUIT FOR A SAUCE TO SERVE WITH SALMON. THE SAUCE WORKS WELL WITH OTHER FISH AND IS ALSO GOOD WITH CHICKEN OR TURKEY.

SERVES FOUR

INGREDIENTS
  6 ripe guavas
  45ml/3 tbsp vegetable oil
  1 small onion, finely chopped
  120ml/4fl oz/½ cup well-flavoured
    chicken stock
  10ml/2 tsp hot pepper sauce
  4 salmon steaks
  salt and ground black pepper
  strips of red (bell) pepper to garnish

COOK'S TIP
Ripe guavas have yellow skin and
succulent flesh that ranges in colour
from white to deep pink or salmon red.
They are exceptionally rich in vitamin C.
Ripe fruit will keep in the refrigerator for
a few days; green guavas will need to be
placed in a warm place until they ripen.

1 Cut each guava in half. Scoop the seeded soft flesh into a strainer set over a bowl. Press it through the strainer, discard the seeds and skin and set the pulp aside.

2 Heat 30ml/2 tbsp of the oil in a frying pan. Cook the chopped onion for about 4 minutes over a moderate heat until softened and translucent.

3 Stir in the guava pulp, with the chicken stock and hot pepper sauce. Cook, stirring constantly, until the sauce thickens. Keep it warm until needed.

4 Brush the salmon steaks on 1 side with a little of the remaining oil. Season them with salt and pepper. Heat a flat or ridged griddle pan until very hot and add the salmon steaks, oiled side down. Cook for 2–3 minutes, until the underside is golden, then brush the surface with oil, turn each salmon steak over and cook the other side until the fish is cooked and flakes easily when tested with the tip of a sharp knife.

5 Transfer each steak to a warmed plate. Serve, garnished with strips of red pepper on a pool of sauce. A fresh green salad is a good accompaniment.

PUEBLO FISH BAKE

THE LIME JUICE IS A PERFECT PARTNER FOR THE TROUT, WHICH IS AN OILY FISH. MARINATING MEANS THAT THE FISH IS BEAUTIFULLY TENDER WHEN COOKED.

SERVES FOUR

INGREDIENTS
    2 fresh pasilla chillies
    4 rainbow trout, cleaned
    4 garlic cloves
    10ml/2 tsp dried oregano
    juice of 2 limes
    50g/2oz/½ cup flaked (sliced) almonds
    salt and ground black pepper

1 Roast the chillies in a dry frying pan or griddle pan until the skins are blistered, being careful not to let the flesh burn. Put them in a strong plastic bag and tie the top to keep the steam in. Set aside for 20 minutes.

2 Meanwhile, rub a little salt into the cavities in the trout, to ensure they are completely clean, then rinse them under cold running water. Drain and pat dry with kitchen paper.

COOK'S TIP
Cooking fish in a paper parcel means that it stays very moist. Trout cooks perfectly by this method, but you could use other fish; try tuna steaks, small mackerel or salmon fillets.

3 Remove the chillies from the bag and peel off the skins. Cut off the stalks, then slit the chillies and scrape out the seeds. Chop the flesh coarsely and put it in a mortar. Crush with a pestle until the mixture forms a paste.

4 Place the chilli paste in a shallow dish that will hold all the trout in a single layer. Slice the garlic along the length of the cloves and add to the dish.

5 Add the oregano and 10ml/2 tsp salt, then stir in the lime juice and pepper to taste. Add the trout, turning to coat them in the mixture. Cover the dish and set aside for at least 30 minutes, turning the trout again halfway through.

6 Preheat the oven to 200°C/400°F/ Gas 6. Have ready 4 pieces of foil, each large enough to wrap a trout. Top each sheet with a piece of greaseproof (waxed) paper of the same size.

7 Place 1 of the trout on 1 of the pieces of paper, moisten with the marinade, then sprinkle about a quarter of the almonds over the top.

8 Bring up the sides of the paper and fold over to seal in the fish, then fold the foil over to make a neat parcel. Make 3 more parcels in the same way, then place them side by side in a large roasting pan.

9 Transfer the parcels to the oven and bake for 25 minutes. Put each parcel on an individual plate, or open them in the kitchen and serve unwrapped if you prefer. This dish goes well with new potatoes and cooked fresh vegetables, and you can garnish it with fresh oregano leaves if you like.

SWORDFISH TACOS

IT IS IMPORTANT NOT TO OVERCOOK SWORDFISH, OR IT CAN BE TOUGH AND DRY. COOKED CORRECTLY, HOWEVER, IT IS ABSOLUTELY DELICIOUS AND MAKES A GREAT CHANGE FROM BEEF OR CHICKEN AS A TACO FILLING.

SERVES SIX

INGREDIENTS
3 swordfish steaks
30ml/2 tbsp vegetable oil
2 garlic cloves, crushed
1 small onion, chopped
3 fresh green chillies, seeded
   and chopped
3 tomatoes
small bunch of fresh coriander
   (cilantro), chopped
6 fresh corn tortillas
½ iceberg lettuce, shredded
salt and ground black pepper
lemon wedges, to serve (optional)

1 Preheat the grill (broiler). Put the swordfish on an oiled rack and grill (broil) for 2–3 minutes on each side. When cool enough to handle, remove the skin and flake the fish into a bowl.

2 Heat the oil in a pan. Add the garlic, onion and chillies and cook for 5 minutes or until the onion is soft and translucent.

3 Cut a cross in the base of each tomato and pour over boiling water. After 3 minutes plunge into cold water. Remove the skins and seeds and chop the flesh into 1cm/½in dice.

4 Add the tomatoes and swordfish to the onion mixture. Cook for 5 minutes over a low heat. Add the coriander and cook for 1–2 minutes. Season to taste.

5 Wrap the tortillas in foil and steam on a plate over boiling water until pliable. Place some shredded lettuce and fish mixture on each tortilla. Fold in half and serve with lemon wedges, if liked.

CHARGRILLED SWORDFISH WITH CHILLI AND LIME SAUCE

SWORDFISH IS A PRIME CANDIDATE FOR THE BARBECUE, SERVED WITH A SPICY SAUCE WHOSE FIRE IS TEMPERED WITH CRÈME FRAÎCHE, AND CHARGRILLED VEGETABLES SUCH AS AUBERGINE.

SERVES FOUR

INGREDIENTS
2 fresh serrano chillies
4 tomatoes
45ml/3 tbsp olive oil
grated rind and juice of 1 lime
4 swordfish steaks
2.5ml/½ tsp salt
2.5ml/½ tsp ground black pepper
175ml/6fl oz/¾ cup crème fraîche

1 Roast the chillies in a dry griddle pan until the skins are blistered. Put in a strong plastic bag, seal and set aside for 20 minutes, then peel off the skins. Cut off the stalks, slit lengthwise, scrape out the seeds and slice the flesh.

2 Cut a cross in the base of each tomato. Place them in a heatproof bowl and pour over boiling water to cover. After 3 minutes, lift the tomatoes out with a slotted spoon and plunge them into a bowl of cold water. Drain. The skins will have begun to peel back from the crosses. Remove all the skin from the tomatoes, then cut them in half and squeeze out the seeds. Chop the flesh into 1cm/½in pieces.

3 Heat 15ml/1 tbsp of the oil in a small pan and add the strips of chilli, with the lime rind and juice. Cook for 2–3 minutes, then stir in the tomatoes. Cook for 10 minutes, stirring the mixture occasionally, until the tomato is pulpy.

4 Brush the swordfish steaks with olive oil and season. Cook on a barbecue or grill (broil) for 3–4 minutes, turning once. Meanwhile, stir the crème fraîche into the sauce, heat it through gently and pour over the swordfish steaks. Serve garnished with fresh parsley.

SALMON WITH TEQUILA CREAM SAUCE

USE REPOSADA TEQUILA, WHICH IS LIGHTLY AGED, FOR THIS SAUCE. IT HAS A SMOOTHER, MORE ROUNDED FLAVOUR, WHICH GOES WELL WITH THE CREAM.

SERVES FOUR

INGREDIENTS
   3 fresh jalapeño chillies
   45ml/3 tbsp olive oil
   1 small onion, finely chopped
   150ml/¼ pint/⅔ cup fish stock
   grated rind and juice of 1 lime
   120ml/4fl oz/½ cup single (light) cream
   30ml/2 tbsp reposada tequila
   1 firm avocado
   4 salmon fillets
   salt and ground white pepper
   strips of green (bell) pepper and
      fresh flat leaf parsley, to garnish

1 Roast the chillies in a frying pan until the skins are blistered, being careful not to let the flesh burn. Put them in a strong plastic bag and tie the top to keep the steam in. Set aside for 20 minutes.

2 Heat 15ml/1 tbsp of the oil in a heavy pan. Add the onion and cook for 3–4 minutes, then add the stock, lime rind and juice. Cook for 10 minutes, until the stock starts to reduce. Remove the chillies from the bag and peel off the skins, slit and scrape out the seeds.

3 Stir the cream into the onion and stock mixture. Slice the chilli flesh into strips and add to the pan. Cook over a gentle heat, stirring constantly, for 2–3 minutes. Season to taste with salt and white pepper.

4 Stir the tequila into the onion and chilli mixture. Leave the pan over a very low heat. Peel the avocado, remove the stone (pit) and slice the flesh. Brush the salmon fillets on 1 side with a little of the remaining oil.

5 Heat a frying pan or ridged griddle pan until very hot and add the salmon, oiled side down. Cook for 2–3 minutes, until the underside is golden, then brush the top with oil, turn each fillet over and cook the other side until the fish is cooked and flakes easily when tested with the tip of a sharp knife.

6 Serve on a pool of sauce, with the avocado slices. Garnish with strips of green pepper and fresh parsley. This is good with Fried Potatoes.

PRAWN SALAD

IN MEXICO, THIS SALAD WOULD FORM THE FISH COURSE IN A FORMAL MEAL, BUT IT IS SO GOOD THAT YOU'LL WANT TO SERVE IT ON ALL SORTS OF OCCASIONS. IT IS PERFECT FOR A BUFFET LUNCH.

SERVES FOUR

INGREDIENTS

450g/1lb/4 cups cooked peeled prawns (shrimp)
juice of 1 lime
3 tomatoes
1 ripe but firm avocado
30ml/2 tbsp hot chilli sauce
5ml/1 tsp sugar
150ml/¼ pint/⅔ cup sour cream
2 Little Gem (Bibb) lettuces
salt and ground black pepper
fresh basil leaves and strips of green (bell) pepper, to garnish

1 Put the prawns in a large bowl, add the lime juice and salt and pepper. Toss lightly, then leave to marinate.

2 Cut a cross in the base of each tomato. Place them in a heatproof bowl and pour over boiling water to cover.

3 After 3 minutes, lift the tomatoes out on a slotted spoon and plunge them into a bowl of cold water. Drain. The skins will have begun to peel back easily from the crosses.

4 Peel the tomatoes completely, then cut them in half and squeeze out the seeds. Chop the flesh into 1cm/½in cubes and add it to the prawns.

5 Cut the avocado in half, remove the skin and seed (pit), then slice the flesh into 1cm/½in chunks. Add it to the prawn and tomato mixture.

6 Mix the hot chilli sauce, sugar and sour cream in a bowl. Fold into the prawn mixture. Line a bowl with the lettuce leaves, then top with the prawn mixture. Cover and chill for at least 1 hour, then garnish with fresh basil and strips of green pepper. Crusty bread makes a perfect accompaniment.

PRAWNS WITH ALMOND SAUCE

GROUND ALMONDS ADD AN INTERESTING TEXTURE TO THE CREAMY, PIQUANT SAUCE THAT ACCOMPANIES THESE PRAWNS.

SERVES SIX

INGREDIENTS
  1 ancho or similar dried chilli
  30ml/2 tbsp vegetable oil
  1 onion, chopped
  3 garlic cloves, coarsely chopped
  8 tomatoes
  5ml/1 tsp ground cumin
  120ml/4floz/½ cup chicken stock
  130g/4½ oz/generous 1 cup
    ground almonds
  175ml/6fl oz/¾ cup crème fraîche
  ½ lime
  900g/2lb/8 cups cooked peeled
    prawns (shrimp)
  salt
  fresh coriander (cilantro) and spring
    onion (scallion) strips, to garnish
  rice and tortillas, to serve

1 Place the dried chilli in a heatproof bowl and pour over boiling water to cover. Leave to soak for 30 minutes until softened. Drain, remove the stalk, then slit the chilli and scrape out the seeds with a small sharp knife. Chop the flesh coarsely and set it aside.

2 Heat the oil in a frying pan and cook the onion and garlic until soft.

VARIATIONS
Try this sauce with other types of fish, too. Adding just a few prawns (shrimp) and serving it over steamed sole would make a very luxurious dish. The sauce is also very good with chicken.

3 Cut a cross in the base of each tomato. Place them in a heatproof bowl and pour over boiling water to cover. After 3 minutes, lift the tomatoes out on a slotted spoon and plunge them into a bowl of cold water. Drain. The skins will have begun to peel back.

4 Peel the tomatoes completely, then cut them in half and scoop out the seeds. Chop the flesh into 1cm/½in cubes and add it to the onion mixture, with the chopped chilli. Stir in the ground cumin and cook for 10 minutes, stirring occasionally.

5 Tip the mixture into a food processor or blender. Add the stock and process on high speed until smooth.

6 Pour the mixture into a large pan, add the ground almonds and stir over a low heat for 2–3 minutes. Gently stir in the crème fraîche until is has been incorporated completely.

7 Squeeze the juice from the lime and stir it into the sauce. Season with salt to taste, then increase the heat and bring the sauce to simmering point.

8 Add the prawns to the pan and heat for 2–3 minutes, depending on size, until warmed through. Serve on a bed of rice, garnished with coriander and spring onion strips, and offer warm tortillas on the side.

CRAB WITH GREEN RICE

THIS IS A POPULAR DISH IN THE WESTERN COASTAL AREAS OF MEXICO. PRAWNS CAN BE USED INSTEAD OF CRAB MEAT IF YOU PREFER AND THE DISH ALSO WORKS WELL WITH WARM CORN TORTILLAS.

SERVES FOUR

INGREDIENTS

225g/8oz/generous 1 cup long grain white rice
500g/1¼lb/3⅓ cups drained canned tomatillos
bunch of fresh coriander (cilantro)
1 onion, coarsely chopped
3 poblano or other fresh green chillies, seeded and chopped
3 garlic cloves
45ml/3 tbsp olive oil
500g/1¼lb/2½ cups crab meat
300ml/½ pint/1¼ cups fish stock
60ml/4 tbsp dry white wine
salt
spring onion (scallion) slices, to garnish

1 Put the rice in a heatproof bowl, pour over boiling water to cover and leave to stand for 20 minutes. Drain thoroughly.

2 Put the tomatillos in a food processor or blender and process until smooth. Chop half the coriander and add to the tomatillo purée, with the onion, chillies and garlic. Process again until smooth.

3 Heat the oil in a large pan. Add the rice and cook over a moderate heat for 5 minutes, until all the oil has been absorbed. Stir occasionally to prevent the rice from sticking.

4 Stir in the tomatillo mixture, with the crab meat, stock and wine. Cover and cook over a low heat for about 20 minutes or until all the liquid has been absorbed. Stir occasionally and add a little more liquid if the rice starts to stick to the pan. Add salt as required, then spoon into a dish and garnish with the remaining coriander and the spring onion slices. Green salad and lime wedges make good accompaniments.

SCALLOPS WITH GARLIC AND CORIANDER

SHELLFISH IS OFTEN COOKED VERY SIMPLY IN MEXICO, HOT CHILLI SAUCE AND LIME BEING POPULAR INGREDIENTS IN MANY FISH RECIPES.

SERVES FOUR

INGREDIENTS
    20 scallops
    2 courgettes (zucchini)
    75g/3oz/6 tbsp butter
    15ml/1 tbsp vegetable oil
    4 garlic cloves, chopped
    30ml/2 tbsp hot chilli sauce
    juice of 1 lime
    small bunch of fresh coriander
        (cilantro), finely chopped

COOK'S TIP
Oil can withstand higher temperatures than butter, but butter gives fried food added flavour. Using a mixture, as here, provides the perfect compromise.

1 If you have bought scallops in their shells, open them. Hold a scallop shell in the palm of your hand, with the flat side uppermost. Insert the blade of a knife close to the hinge that joins the shells and prise them apart. Run the blade of the knife across the inside of the flat shell to cut away the scallop. Only the white adductor muscle and the orange coral are eaten, so pull away and discard all other parts. Rinse the scallops under cold running water.

2 Cut the courgettes in half, then into 4 pieces. Melt the butter in the oil in a large frying pan. Add the courgettes and cook until soft. Remove from the pan. Add the garlic and cook until golden. Stir in the hot chilli sauce.

3 Add the scallops to the sauce. Cook, stirring constantly, for 1–2 minutes only. Stir in the lime juice, chopped coriander and the courgette pieces. Serve immediately on heated plates.

Vegetable Dishes

Many familiar vegetables and fruits are grown in Mexico, including green beans, tomatoes, cabbages, cauliflowers, and onions, and the vegetable content of the main meal will often be a course in between the soup and the meat course. Vegetables are also used as an accompaniment, and the chilli content of the dish will reflect this, with just a hint of chilli flavour to add some interest. As in Mexican fish dishes, chilli is used in vegetable dishes with a delicate hand, so that the taste of the fresh vegetable is not overpowered, and the result is a range of dishes that makes the most of fresh ingredients and subtle flavourings.

MEXICAN-STYLE GREEN PEAS

THIS IS A DELICIOUS WAY OF COOKING FRESH PEAS, AND MAKES AN EXCELLENT ACCOMPANIMENT TO ANY MEAL. THE FLAVOUR COMES FROM THE VEGETABLES THEMSELVES, SO USE VINE TOMATOES AND ORGANIC PEAS IF POSSIBLE.

SERVES FOUR

INGREDIENTS
2 tomatoes
50g/2oz/¼ cup butter
2 garlic cloves, halved
1 medium onion, halved and
  thinly sliced
400g/14oz/scant 3 cups shelled
  fresh peas
30ml/2 tbsp water
salt and ground black pepper
fresh chives, to garnish

1 Cut a cross in the base of each tomato. Place the tomatoes in a heatproof bowl and pour over boiling water to cover. Leave them in the water for 3 minutes, then lift the tomatoes out on a slotted spoon and plunge them into a bowl of cold water. Drain. The skins will have begun to peel back.

2 Remove the skins completely, then cut the tomatoes in half and scoop out the seeds. Chop the flesh into 1cm/½in dice.

3 Melt the butter in a pan. Cook the garlic until golden. Do not overcook or it will add a bitter taste. Lift it out on a slotted spoon and discard it. Add the onion slices to the pan and cook until transparent.

4 Add the tomato to the onion, mix well, then stir in the peas. Pour over the water, lower the heat and cover the pan tightly. Cook for 10 minutes, shaking the pan occasionally to stop the mixture from sticking to the base.

5 Check that the peas are cooked, then season with plenty of salt and pepper. Transfer the mixture to a heated dish and serve, garnished with fresh chives.

MUSHROOMS WITH CHIPOTLE CHILLIES

CHIPOTLE CHILLIES ARE JALAPEÑOS THAT HAVE BEEN SMOKE-DRIED. THEIR SMOKY FLAVOUR IS THE PERFECT FOIL FOR THE MUSHROOMS IN THIS SIMPLE DISH.

SERVES SIX

INGREDIENTS
2 chipotle chillies
450g/1lb/6 cups button
  (white) mushrooms
60ml/4 tbsp vegetable oil
1 onion, finely chopped
2 garlic cloves, crushed or chopped
salt
small bunch of fresh coriander
  (cilantro), to garnish

COOK'S TIP
Baby button (white) mushrooms are perfect for this dish, if you can get them. You can, of course, use any white mushrooms, but larger ones may be better halved or quartered.

1 Soak the dried chillies in a bowl of hot water for about 10 minutes until they are softened. Drain, cut off the stalks, then slit the chillies and scrape out the seeds. Chop the flesh finely.

2 Trim the mushrooms, then clean them with a damp cloth or kitchen paper. If they are large, cut them in half.

3 Heat the oil in a large frying pan. Add the onion, garlic, chillies and mushrooms and stir until coated in the oil. Cook for 6–8 minutes, stirring occasionally, until the onion and is cooked. Season to taste and spoon into a serving dish. Chop some of the coriander, leaving some whole leaves, and use to garnish. Serve hot.

STUFFED CHILLIES <u>IN A</u> WALNUT SAUCE

THE POTATO AND MEAT FILLING IN THESE CHILLIES IS A GOOD PARTNER FOR THE RICH, CREAMY SAUCE THAT COVERS THEM.

SERVES FOUR

INGREDIENTS
  8 ancho chillies
  1 large potato, about 200g/7oz
  45ml/3 tbsp vegetable oil
  115g/4oz lean minced (ground) pork
  1 onion, chopped
  5ml/1 tsp ground cinnamon
  115g/4oz/1 cup walnuts,
    coarsely chopped
  50g/2oz/½ cup chopped almonds
  150g/5oz/⅔ cup cream cheese
  50g/2oz/½ cup soft goat's cheese
  120ml/4fl oz/½ cup single
    (light) cream
  120ml/4fl oz/½ cup dry sherry
  50g/2oz/½ cup plain (all-
    purpose) flour
  2.5ml/½ tsp ground white pepper
  2 eggs, separated
  oil, for deep-frying
  salt
  chopped fresh herbs, to garnish

1 Soak the dried chillies in a bowl of hot water for 30 minutes until softened. Drain, cut off the stalks, then slit them down 1 side. Scrape out the seeds.

2 Peel the potato and cut it into 1cm/½in cubes. Heat 15ml/1 tbsp of the oil in a large frying pan, add the pork and cook, stirring constantly, until it has browned evenly.

COOK'S TIP
The potatoes must not break or become too floury. Do not overcook. For the best results buy waxy potatoes.

3 Add the potato cubes and mix well. Cover and cook over a low heat for 25–30 minutes, stirring occasionally. Do not worry if the potato sticks to the base of the pan. Season with salt, remove from the heat and set aside.

4 Heat the remaining oil in a separate frying pan and cook the onion with the cinnamon for 3–4 minutes or until softened. Stir in the nuts and cook for 3–4 minutes more.

5 Add both types of cheese to the pan, with the cream and sherry. Mix well. Reduce the heat to the lowest setting and cook until the cheese melts and the sauce starts to thicken. Taste and season if necessary.

6 Spread out the flour on a plate or in a shallow dish. Season with the white pepper. Beat the egg yolks in a bowl until they are pale and thick.

7 In a separate, grease-free bowl, whisk the whites until they form soft peaks. Add a generous pinch of salt, then fold in the yolks, a little at a time.

8 Spoon some of the filling into each chilli. Pat the outside dry with kitchen paper. Heat the oil for deep-frying to a temperature of 180°C/350°F.

9 Coat a chilli in flour, then dip it in the egg batter, covering it completely. Drain for a few seconds, then add to the hot oil. Add several more battered chillies, but do not overcrowd the pan. Fry the chillies until golden, then drain on kitchen paper and keep hot while cooking successive batches.

10 Reheat the sauce over a low heat, if necessary. Arrange the chillies on individual plates, spoon a little sauce over each and serve immediately, sprinkled with chopped fresh herbs. A green salad goes well with this dish.

POTATOES WITH CHORIZO AND GREEN CHILLIES

MEXICANS MAKE THEIR OWN CHORIZO SAUSAGE, SOMETIMES USING IT FRESH, BUT ALSO PUTTING IT INTO CASINGS TO DRY, WHEN IT RESEMBLES THE SPANISH VERSION WHICH IS NOW POPULAR THE WORLD OVER. THIS RECIPE MAKES A DELICIOUS BRUNCH DISH. TYPICAL OF PEASANT FOOD, IT IS BASED ON THE COMBINATION OF PLENTY OF POTATO MIXED WITH STRONGLY FLAVOURED MEAT TO HELP IT GO FURTHER.

SERVES FOUR TO SIX

INGREDIENTS
900g/2lb potatoes, peeled and diced
30ml/2 tbsp vegetable oil
2 garlic cloves, crushed
4 spring onions (scallions), chopped
2 fresh jalapeño chillies, seeded
  and diced
300g/11oz chorizo sausage, skinned
150g/5oz/1¼ cups grated Monterey
  Jack or Cheddar cheese
salt (optional)

1 Bring a large pan of water to the boil and add the potatoes. When the water returns to the boil, lower the heat and simmer the potatoes for 5 minutes. Tip the potatoes into a colander and drain them thoroughly.

COOK'S TIP
Use firm-textured potatoes, such as Desiree, Pentland Dell or Estima, for this dish. If you can't locate Monterey Jack, look out for a mature (sharp) Gouda, or use a mild Cheddar.

2 Heat the oil in a large frying pan, add the garlic, spring onions and chillies and cook for 3–4 minutes. Add the diced potato and cook until the cubes begin to brown a little.

3 Cut the chorizo into small cubes and add these to the pan. Cook the mixture for 5 minutes more, until the sausage has heated through.

4 Season with salt if necessary, then add the cheese. Mix quickly and carefully, trying not to break up the cubes of potato. Serve immediately, while the cheese is still melting.

RED CAULIFLOWER

VEGETABLES ARE SELDOM SERVED PLAIN IN MEXICO. THE CAULIFLOWER HERE IS FLAVOURED WITH A SIMPLE TOMATO SALSA AND FRESH CHEESE. THE SALSA COULD BE ANY TABLE SALSA; TOMATILLO IS PARTICULARLY GOOD. THE CONTRAST WITH THE TEXTURE AND MILD FLAVOUR OF THE CAULIFLOWER MAKES FOR A TASTY DISH.

SERVES SIX

INGREDIENTS

1 small onion
1 lime
1 medium cauliflower
400g/14oz can chopped tomatoes
4 fresh serrano chillies, seeded and
 finely chopped
1.5ml/¼ tsp caster (superfine) sugar
75g/3oz feta cheese, crumbled
salt
chopped fresh flat leaf parsley,
 to garnish

COOK'S TIP
Use a zester for the lime, if have you have one. This handy little tool enables you to pare off tiny strips of the rind, leaving the pith behind.

1 Chop the onion very finely and place in a bowl. With a zester peel away the rind of the lime in thin strips. Add to the chopped onion.

2 Cut the lime in half and add the juice from both halves to the onion and lime rind mixture. Set aside so that the lime juice can soften the onion. Cut the cauliflower into florets.

3 Tip the tomatoes into a pan and add the chillies and sugar. Heat gently. Meanwhile, place the cauliflower in a pan of boiling water and cook gently for 5–8 minutes until tender.

4 Add the onion to the tomato salsa, with salt to taste, stir in and heat through, then spoon about a third of the salsa into a serving dish.

5 Arrange the drained cauliflower florets on top of the salsa and spoon the remaining salsa on top.

6 Sprinkle with the feta, which should soften a little on contact. Serve immediately, sprinkled with chopped fresh flat leaf parsley.

GREEN LIMA BEANS IN A SAUCE

MAKE THE MOST OF LIMA BEANS OR BROAD BEANS BY TEAMING THEM WITH TOMATOES AND FRESH CHILLIES IN THIS SIMPLE ACCOMPANIMENT.

SERVES FOUR

INGREDIENTS

450g/1lb fresh lima beans or
    broad beans
30ml/2 tbsp olive oil
1 onion, finely chopped
2 garlic cloves, crushed
400g/14oz can plum tomatoes,
    drained and chopped
25g/1oz/about 3 tbsp drained pickled
    jalapeño chilli slices, chopped
salt
fresh coriander (cilantro) and lemon
    slices, to garnish

COOK'S TIP
Pickled chillies are often hotter than
roasted chillies – taste one before adding
to the recipe and adjust the quantity to
suit your taste.

1 Bring a pan of lightly salted water to
the boil. Add the lima beans or broad
beans and cook for 15 minutes, or until
just tender.

2 Meanwhile, heat the olive oil in a
frying pan, add the onion and garlic and
sauté until the onion is translucent. Tip
in the tomatoes and continue to cook,
stirring, until the mixture thickens.

3 Add the chilli slices and cook for
1–2 minutes. Season with salt to taste.

4 Drain the beans and return them to
the pan. Pour over the tomato mixture
and stir over the heat for a few minutes.
If the sauce thickens too quickly, add a
little water. Spoon into a serving dish,
garnish with the coriander and lemon
slices and serve.

GREEN BEANS WITH EGGS

THIS IS AN UNUSUAL WAY OF COOKING GREEN BEANS, BUT TASTES DELICIOUS. TRY THIS DISH FOR A LIGHT SUPPER OR AS AN ACCOMPANIMENT TO A SIMPLE ROAST.

SERVES SIX

INGREDIENTS

300g/11oz green beans, trimmed
    and halved
30ml/2 tbsp vegetable oil
1 onion, halved and
    thinly sliced
3 eggs
salt and ground black pepper
50g/2oz/½ cup grated Monterey Jack
    or mild Cheddar cheese
strips of lemon rind, to garnish

VARIATION
Freshly grated Parmesan can be used
instead of the Monterey Jack or Cheddar
cheese for a sharper flavour.

1 Bring a pan of water to the boil, add
the beans and cook for 5–6 minutes or
until tender. Drain the beans in a
colander, rinse under cold water to
preserve the bright green colour, then
drain once again.

2 Heat the oil in a frying pan and cook
the onion slices for 3–4 minutes until
soft and translucent. Break the eggs
into a bowl and beat with seasoning.

3 Add the egg mixture to the onion.
Cook slowly over a moderate heat,
stirring constantly so that the egg is
lightly scrambled. The egg should be
moist throughout. Do not overcook.

4 Add the beans to the pan and cook
for a few minutes until warmed through.
Tip the mixture into a heated serving
dish, sprinkle with the grated cheese
and lemon rind and serve.

COURGETTES WITH CHEESE AND GREEN CHILLIES

THIS IS A VERY TASTY WAY TO SERVE COURGETTES, OFTEN A RATHER BLAND VEGETABLE, AND THE DISH LOOKS GOOD TOO. SERVE IT AS A VEGETARIAN MAIN DISH OR AN UNUSUAL SIDE DISH.

SERVES SIX AS AN ACCOMPANIMENT

INGREDIENTS
    30ml/2 tbsp vegetable oil
    ½ onion, thinly sliced
    2 garlic cloves, crushed
    5ml/1 tsp dried oregano
    2 tomatoes
    500g/1¼lb courgettes (zucchini)
    50g/2oz/⅓ cup drained pickled
      jalapeño chilli slices, chopped
    115g/4oz/½ cup cream
      cheese, cubed
    salt and ground black pepper
    fresh oregano sprigs, to garnish

1 Heat the oil in a frying pan. Add the onion, garlic and dried oregano. Cook for 3–4 minutes, until the onion is soft and translucent.

2 Cut a cross in the base of each tomato. Place in a heatproof bowl and cover with boiling water. Leave in the water for 3 minutes, then lift out on a slotted spoon and plunge into a bowl of cold water. Drain. The skins will have begun to peel back from the crosses. Remove the skins, cut the tomatoes in half and squeeze out the seeds. Chop the flesh into strips.

3 Trim the courgettes, then cut them lengthways into 1cm/½in wide strips. Slice the strips into thin sticks.

4 Stir the courgettes into the onion mixture and cook for 10 minutes, stirring occasionally, until just tender. Add the tomatoes and jalapeños and cook for 2–3 minutes more.

5 Add the cream cheese. Reduce the heat to the lowest setting. As the cheese melts, stir gently to coat the courgettes. Season to taste, pile into a heated dish and serve, garnished with fresh oregano. If serving as a main dish, rustic bread makes a good accompaniment.

COURGETTE TORTE

This dish looks rather like a Spanish omelette, which is traditionally served at room temperature. Serve warm or prepare it in advance and leave to cool, but do not chill.

2 Slice the onion and add it to the oil remaining in the pan, with most of the jalapeño strips, reserving some for the garnish. Cook until the onion has softened and are golden. Using a slotted spoon, add the onion and jalapeños to the courgettes.

3 Beat the eggs in a large bowl. Add the flour, cheese and cayenne. Mix well, then stir in the courgette mixture, with salt to taste.

4 Grease a 23cm/9in round shallow ovenproof dish with the butter. Pour in the courgette mixture and bake for 30 minutes until risen, firm to the touch and golden. Leave to cool.

5 Serve the courgette torte in thick wedges, sprinkled with black pepper and garnished with the remaining jalapeño strips, and chives if you like. A tomato salad, sprinkled with chives, makes a colourful accompaniment.

SERVES FOUR TO SIX

INGREDIENTS
  500g/1¼lb courgettes (zucchini)
  60ml/4 tbsp vegetable oil
  1 small onion
  3 fresh jalapeño chillies, seeded and
    cut in strips
  3 large (US extra large) eggs
  50g/2oz/½ cup self-raising (self-
    rising) flour
  115g/4oz/1 cup grated Monterey Jack
    or mild Cheddar cheese
  2.5ml/½ tsp cayenne pepper
  15g/½oz/1 tbsp butter
  salt and ground black pepper
  chopped chives, to garnish (optional)

1 Preheat the oven to 180°C/350°F/ Gas 4. Trim the courgettes, then slice them thinly. Heat the oil in a large frying pan. Add the courgettes and cook for a few minutes, turning them over at least once, until they are soft and beginning to brown. Using a slotted spoon, transfer them to a bowl.

PUMPKIN WITH SPICES

ROASTED PUMPKIN HAS A WONDERFUL RICH, SWEET FLAVOUR. YOU CAN EAT IT STRAIGHT FROM THE SKIN, EAT THE SKIN TOO, OR SCOOP OUT THE COOKED FLESH, ADD A SPOONFUL OF SALSA AND WRAP IT IN A WARM TORTILLA.

SERVES SIX

INGREDIENTS
   1kg/2¼lb pumpkin
   50g/2oz/¼ cup butter, melted
   10ml/2 tsp hot chilli sauce
   2.5ml/½ tsp salt
   2.5ml/½ tsp ground allspice
   5ml/1 tsp ground cinnamon
   chopped fresh herbs, to garnish
   Classic Tomato Salsa and crème
      fraîche, to serve

COOK'S TIP
Green, grey or orange-skinned pumpkins all roast well. The orange-fleshed varieties are the most colourful when it comes to cooking.

1 Preheat the oven to 220°C/425°F/ Gas 7. Cut the pumpkin into large pieces. Scoop out and discard the fibre and seeds, then put the pumpkin pieces in a roasting pan.

2 Mix the melted butter and chilli sauce and drizzle the mixture evenly over the pumpkin pieces.

3 Put the salt in a small bowl and add the ground allspice and cinnamon. Sprinkle the mixture over the pumpkin.

4 Roast for 25 minutes or until the pumpkin flesh yields when pressed gently. Serve on a heated platter and offer the tomato salsa and crème fraîche separately.

FRIJOLES CHARROS

THESE "COWBOY BEANS" TASTE RATHER LIKE BOSTON BAKED BEANS, BUT WITH A BIT MORE PUNCH.
THE FLAVOUR IMPROVES ON KEEPING, SO MAKE IT THE DAY BEFORE YOU INTEND TO SERVE IT.

SERVES SIX

INGREDIENTS

   2 x 400g/14oz cans pinto beans
   120ml/4fl oz/½ cup Mexican beer
   115g/4oz/⅔ cup drained pickled
     jalapeño chilli slices, chopped
   2 tomatoes, peeled and chopped
   5ml/1 tsp ground cinnamon
   175g/6oz streaky (fatty) bacon
   1 onion, chopped
   2 garlic cloves, crushed
   175g/6oz rindless smoked lean
     bacon, diced
   45ml/3 tbsp soft dark brown sugar
   wheat flour tortillas, to serve

1 Put the drained pinto beans in a pan. Stir in the beer and cook over a high heat for 5 minutes, until some of the beer has evaporated.

2 Lower the heat slightly and stir in the chopped jalapeño chilli, then add the tomatoes and cinnamon. Continue to cook, stirring occasionally, for about 10 minutes.

3 Meanwhile, heat the bacon in a frying pan until the fat runs. The quantity suggested should yield about 45ml/3 tbsp bacon fat.

4 Discard the bacon, then add the onion and garlic to the pan and cook for about 5 minutes, until browned. Using a slotted spoon, lift out the garlic and onion and stir them into the beans.

5 Add the diced smoked bacon to the fat remaining in the frying pan and fry until crisp. Add the bacon and any remaining fat to the beans and mix well.

6 Stir in the sugar. Cook the bean and bacon mixture over a low heat, stirring constantly, until the sugar is dissolved. Serve immediately or spoon into a bowl, leave to cool, cover, then chill for reheating next day. Serve with warmed wheat flour tortillas.

FRIED PLANTAIN

THESE ARE THE PERFECT ACCOMPANIMENT TO HIGHLY SPICED AND SEASONED FOODS. THEIR SWEET FLAVOUR PROVIDES AN INTERESTING CONTRAST.

SERVES FOUR

INGREDIENTS
4 ripe plantains
75g/3oz/6 tbsp butter
10ml/2 tsp vegetable oil
strips of spring onion (scallion) and
red (bell) pepper, to garnish

COOK'S TIP
Ripe plantains have dark, almost black skins. Do not use under-ripe plantains, which are very hard and do not soften on cooking.

1 Peel the plantains, cut them in half along their length, then cut them in half again. Melt the butter with the oil in a large frying pan.

2 Add the plantains to the pan in a single layer and fry for 8–10 minutes, turning halfway through. Spoon into a heated dish and serve, garnished with strips of spring onion and red pepper.

FRIED POTATOES

THESE MAKE THE PERFECT ACCOMPANIMENT FOR CHORIZO, AND ALSO GO VERY WELL WITH EGGS AND BACON.

SERVES FOUR

INGREDIENTS
6 fresh jalapeño chillies
60ml/4 tbsp vegetable oil
1 onion, finely chopped
450g/1lb waxy potatoes, scrubbed
and cut in 1cm/½in cubes
few sprigs of fresh oregano, chopped,
plus extra sprigs, to garnish
75g/3oz/1 cup freshly grated
Parmesan cheese (optional)

1 Dry roast the jalapeños in a griddle pan, turning them frequently so that the skins blacken but do not burn. Place them in a strong plastic bag and tie the top to keep the steam in. Set aside for 20 minutes.

2 Remove the jalapeños from the bag, peel off the skins and remove any stems. Cut them in half, scrape out the seeds, then chop the flesh finely.

COOK'S TIP
If your frying pan does not have a lid, use foil instead.

3 Meanwhile, heat half the oil in a large heavy frying pan which has a lid. Add the chopped onion and cook, stirring occasionally, for 3–4 minutes, until translucent, then add the potato cubes.

4 Stir to coat the potato cubes in oil, then cover the pan and cook over a moderate heat for 20–25 minutes, until the potatoes are tender. Shake the pan occasionally to stop them from sticking to the base.

5 When the potatoes are tender, push them to the side of the frying pan, then add the remaining oil.

6 When the oil is hot, spread out the potatoes again and add the chopped jalapeños. Cook over a high heat for 5–10 minutes, stirring carefully so that the potatoes turn golden brown all over but do not break up.

7 Add the chopped oregano, with the grated Parmesan, if using. Mix gently, spoon on to a heated serving dish and garnish with extra oregano sprigs. Serve as part of a cooked breakfast or brunch.

CORN WITH CREAM

THE TRADITIONAL MEXICAN VERSION OF THIS DISH USES CREAM RATHER THAN SOFT CHEESE, BUT THE FULL-FAT SOFT CHEESE USED HERE GIVES THE SAUCE AN EXCELLENT CONSISTENCY.

SERVES SIX AS A SIDE DISH

INGREDIENTS
  4 corn cobs
  50g/2oz/¼ cup butter
  1 small onion, finely chopped
  115g/4oz/⅔ cup drained pickled
    jalapeño chilli slices
  130g/4½oz/⅔ cup full-fat soft cheese
  25g/1oz/⅓ cup freshly grated
    Parmesan cheese, plus shavings,
    to garnish
  salt and ground black pepper

1 Strip off the husks from the corn and pull off the silks. Place the cobs in a bowl of water and use a vegetable brush to remove any remaining silks. Stand each cob in turn on a board and slice off the kernels, cutting as close to the cob as possible.

2 Melt the butter in a heavy pan, add the chopped onion and cook for 4–5 minutes, stirring occasionally, until the onion has softened and is translucent.

3 Add the corn kernels and cook for 4–5 minutes, until they are just tender. Chop the jalapeños finely and stir them into the corn mixture.

4 Stir in the soft cheese and the grated Parmesan. Cook over a low heat until both cheeses have melted and the corn kernels are coated in the mixture. Season to taste, tip into a heated dish and serve, topped with Parmesan shavings.

VARIATION
A simple version of this dish is sold on street stalls in Mexico. Whole cooked corn cobs are dipped in double (heavy) cream, then sprinkled with crumbled fresh cheese. Next time you cook on a barbecue, try this as an appetizer. Alternatively, bake whole cobs in a shallow dish in an oven preheated to 200°C/400°F/Gas 6 for 30 minutes, until tender and golden. Pour over 120ml/4fl oz/½ cup sour cream or crème fraîche, then sprinkle the cobs with 30ml/2 tbsp freshly grated Parmesan cheese and serve. The corn can also be buttered and grilled (broiled), but there must be plenty of room below the heat.

FRIJOLES DE OLLA

TRAVELLERS OFTEN SAY THAT "BEANS IN A POT", AS IT IS TRANSLATED, TASTE DIFFERENT IN MEXICO FROM THOSE COOKED ANYWHERE ELSE. THE SECRET IS, QUITE LITERALLY, IN THE POT. TRADITIONALLY, CLAY POTS ARE USED, WHICH GIVE THE BEANS A WONDERFUL, SLIGHTLY EARTHY FLAVOUR. THIS DISH WOULD BE SERVED AS JUST ONE OF THE COURSES IN A FORMAL MEXICAN MEAL.

SERVES FOUR

INGREDIENTS
  250g/9oz/1¼ cups dried pinto beans,
    soaked overnight in water to cover
  1.75 litres/3 pints/7½ cups water
  2 onions
  10 garlic cloves, peeled and
    left whole
  bunch of fresh coriander (cilantro)
  salt
For the toppings
  2 fresh red fresno chillies
  1 tomato, peeled and chopped
  2 spring onions (scallions), chopped
  60ml/4 tbsp sour cream
  50g/2oz feta cheese

COOK'S TIP
When cooking dried beans, salt should never be added until afterwards, as it inhibits the softening process.

1 Drain the beans, rinse them under cold water and drain again. Put the water in a large pan, bring to the boil and add the beans.

2 Cut the onions in half and add them to the pan, with the whole garlic cloves. Bring to the boil again, then lower the heat and simmer for 1½ hours, until the beans are tender and there is only a little liquid remaining.

3 While the beans are cooking, prepare the toppings. Spear the chillies on a long-handled metal skewer and roast them over the flame of a gas burner until the skins blister and darken. Do not let the flesh burn. Alternatively, dry-fry them in a griddle pan until the skins are scorched. Put the roasted chillies in a strong plastic bag and tie the top immediately to keep the steam in. Set aside for 20 minutes.

4 Remove the chillies from the bag and peel off the skins. Cut off the stalks, then slit the chillies and scrape out the seeds. Cut the flesh into thin strips and put it in a bowl. Spoon all the other toppings into separate bowls.

5 Ladle about 250ml/8fl oz/1 cup of the beans and liquid into a food processor or blender. Process to a smooth purée. If you prefer, simply mash the beans with a potato masher.

6 Return the bean purée to the pan, and stir it in. Chop the coriander, reserving some leaves to garnish, season with salt and mix well. Ladle the beans into warmed individual bowls and take them to the table with the toppings.

7 Serve the beans with the toppings and add coriander to garnish. Traditionally, each guest spoons a little of the chillies, tomatoes and spring onions over the beans, then adds a spoonful of sour cream. The finishing touch is a little feta cheese, crumbled over each portion.

GREEN RICE

THIS RICE SELDOM FEATURES ON MENUS IN MEXICAN RESTAURANTS, BUT IS OFTEN MADE IN THE HOME. EXTRA CHILLIES AND GREEN PEPPER CAN BE DICED AND ADDED AT THE END, IF YOU LIKE.

SERVES FOUR

INGREDIENTS
    2 fresh green chillies,
      preferably poblanos
    1 small green (bell) pepper
    200g/7oz/1 cup long grain white rice
    1 garlic clove, coarsely chopped
    bunch of fresh coriander (cilantro)
    small bunch of fresh flat leaf parsley
    475ml/16fl oz/2 cups chicken stock
    30ml/2 tbsp vegetable oil
    1 small onion, finely chopped
    salt

1 Dry roast the chillies and green pepper in a griddle pan, turning them frequently so that the skins blacken but the flesh does not burn. Place them in a strong plastic bag, tie the top securely and set aside for 20 minutes.

2 Put the rice in a heatproof bowl, pour over boiling water to cover and leave to stand for 20 minutes.

3 Drain the rice, rinse well under cold water and drain again. Remove the chillies and pepper from the bag and peel off the skins. Remove any stalks, then slit the vegetables and scrape out the seeds with a sharp knife.

4 Put the roasted vegetables in a food processor, with the garlic. Strip off the leaves from the coriander and parsley stalks, reserve some for the garnish and add the rest to the processor. Pour in half the chicken stock and process until smooth. Add the rest of the stock and process the purée again.

5 Heat the oil in a pan, add the onion and rice and fry for 5 minutes over a moderate heat until the rice is golden and the onion translucent. Stir in the purée. Lower the heat, cover and cook for 25–30 minutes or until all the liquid is absorbed and the rice is just tender. Add salt and garnish with the reserved herbs. Served with lime wedges, this rice goes extremely well with fish.

YELLOW RICE

THIS RICE DISH OWES ITS STRIKING COLOUR AND DISTINCTIVE FLAVOUR TO GROUND ACHIOTE SEED, WHICH IS DERIVED FROM ANNATTO. SPRINKLE EXTRA OVER THE DISH AT THE TABLE, IF YOU LIKE.

SERVES SIX

INGREDIENTS
    200g/7oz/1 cup long grain white rice
    30ml/2 tbsp vegetable oil
    5ml/1 tsp ground achiote seed
      (annatto powder)
    1 small onion, finely chopped
    2 garlic cloves, crushed
    475ml/16fl oz/2 cups chicken stock
    50g/2oz/⅓ cup drained pickled
      jalapeño chilli slices, chopped
    salt
    fresh coriander (cilantro) leaves,
      to garnish

COOK'S TIP
Achiote, the seed of the annatto tree, is used as a food colouring and flavouring throughout Latin America. Buy it in spice stores and ethnic food stores. It may be labelled annatto powder.

1 Put the rice in a heatproof bowl, pour over boiling water to cover and leave to stand for 20 minutes. Drain, rinse under cold water and drain again.

2 Heat the oil in a pan, add the ground achiote seed and cook for 2–3 minutes. Add the onion and garlic and cook for a further 3–4 minutes or until the onion is translucent. Stir in the rice and cook for 5 minutes.

3 Pour in the stock, mix well and bring to the boil. Lower the heat, cover the pan with a tight-fitting lid and simmer for 25–30 minutes, until all the liquid has been absorbed.

4 Add the chopped jalapeños to the pan and stir to distribute them evenly. Add salt to taste, then spoon into a heated serving dish and garnish with the fresh coriander leaves. Serve immediately.

CHAYOTES WITH CORN AND CHILLIES

Shaped like pears or avocados, chayotes are members of the squash family and have rather a bland taste. However, they marry extremely well with other ingredients, such as the corn and roasted jalapeños in this medley.

SERVES SIX

INGREDIENTS
  4 fresh jalapeño chillies
  3 *chayotes*
  oil, for frying
  1 red onion, finely chopped
  3 garlic cloves, crushed
  225g/8oz/1⅓ cups sweetcorn kernels,
    thawed if frozen
  150g/5oz/⅔ cup cream cheese
  salt to taste
  25g/1oz/⅓ cup freshly grated
    Parmesan cheese

1 Dry roast the fresh jalapeño chillies in a griddle pan, turning them frequently so that the skins blacken but do not burn. Place them in a plastic bag, tie the top securely, and set them aside for 20 minutes.

2 Meanwhile, peel the *chayotes*, cut them in half and remove the seed from each of them. Cut the flesh into 1cm/½in cubes.

COOK'S TIP
Chayotes go by several names, including *christophene* and *choko*. Store them in a plastic bag in the refrigerator and they will keep for up to 1 month.

3 Heat the oil in a frying pan. Add the onion, garlic, *chayote* cubes and sweetcorn. Cook over a moderate heat for 10 minutes, stirring occasionally.

4 Remove the jalapeños from the bag, peel off the skins and remove any stems. Cut them in half, scrape out the seeds, then cut the flesh into strips.

5 Add the chillies and cream cheese to the pan, stirring gently, until the cheese melts. Season with salt, if needed.

6 Spoon the mixture into a warmed serving dish, sprinkle with Parmesan cheese and serve. This makes a good accompaniment for cold roast meats.

SPINACH SALAD

YOUNG SPINACH LEAVES MAKE A WELCOME CHANGE FROM LETTUCE AND ARE EXCELLENT IN SALADS.
THE ROASTED GARLIC IS AN INSPIRED ADDITION TO THE DRESSING.

SERVES SIX

INGREDIENTS
    500g/1¼lb baby spinach leaves
    50g/2oz/⅓ cup sesame seeds
    50g/2oz/¼ cup butter
    30ml/2 tbsp olive oil
    6 shallots, sliced
    8 fresh serrano chillies, seeded and
      cut into strips
    4 tomatoes, sliced
For the dressing
    6 roasted garlic cloves
    120ml/4fl oz/½ cup white
      wine vinegar
    2.5ml/½ tsp ground white pepper
    1 bay leaf
    2.5ml/½ tsp ground allspice
    30ml/2 tbsp chopped fresh thyme,
      plus extra sprigs, to garnish

COOK'S TIP
To roast individual garlic cloves simply place in a roasting pan in a moderate oven for about 15 minutes until soft.

1 Make the dressing. Remove the skins from the garlic when cool, then chop and combine with the vinegar, pepper, bay leaf, allspice and chopped thyme in a jar with a screw-top lid. Close the lid tightly, shake well, then put the dressing in the refrigerator until needed.

2 Wash the spinach leaves and dry them in a salad spinner or clean dishtowel. Put them in a plastic bag in the refrigerator.

3 Toast the sesame seeds in a dry frying pan, shaking frequently over a moderate heat until golden. Set aside.

4 Heat the butter and oil in a frying pan. Cook the shallots for 4–5 minutes, until softened, then stir in the chilli strips and cook for 2–3 minutes more.

5 In a large bowl, layer the spinach with the shallot and chilli mixture, and the tomato slices. Pour over the dressing. Sprinkle with sesame seeds and serve, garnished with thyme sprigs.

CHAYOTE SALAD

COOL AND REFRESHING, THIS SALAD IS IDEAL ON ITS OWN OR WITH FISH OR CHICKEN DISHES. THE SOFT FLESH OF THE CHAYOTES ABSORBS THE FLAVOUR OF THE DRESSING BEAUTIFULLY.

SERVES FOUR

INGREDIENTS
   2 *chayotes*
   2 firm tomatoes
   1 small onion, finely chopped
   finely sliced strips of fresh red and
      green chilli, to garnish
For the dressing
   2.5ml/½ tsp Dijon mustard
   2.5ml/½ tsp ground anise
   90ml/6 tbsp white wine vinegar
   60ml/4 tbsp olive oil
   salt and ground black pepper

1 Bring a pan of water to the boil. Peel the *chayotes*, cut them in half and remove the seeds. Add them to the boiling water. Lower the heat and simmer for 20 minutes or until the *chayotes* are tender. Drain and set them aside to cool.

2 Meanwhile, peel the tomatoes. Cut a cross in the base of each tomato. Place them in a heatproof bowl and pour over boiling water to cover. After 3 minutes, lift the tomatoes out on a slotted spoon and plunge them into a bowl of cold water. Drain. The skins will have begun to peel back from the crosses. Remove the skins completely and cut the tomatoes into wedges.

3 Make the dressing by combining all the ingredients in a screw-top jar. Close the lid tightly and shake the jar vigorously.

4 Cut the *chayotes* into wedges and place in a bowl with the tomato and onion. Pour over the dressing and serve garnished with strips of fresh red and green chilli.

JICAMA, CHILLI AND LIME SALAD

A VERY TASTY, CRISP VEGETABLE, THE JICAMA IS SOMETIMES CALLED THE MEXICAN POTATO. UNLIKE POTATO, HOWEVER, IT CAN BE EATEN RAW AS WELL AS COOKED. THIS MAKES A GOOD SALAD OR AN APPETIZER TO SERVE WITH DRINKS.

SERVES FOUR

INGREDIENTS
1 *jicama*
2.5ml/½ tsp salt
2 fresh serrano chillies
2 limes

COOK'S TIP
Look for *jicama* in Asian supermarkets, as it is widely used in Chinese cooking. It goes by several names and you may find it labelled as either yam bean or Chinese turnip.

1 Peel the *jicama* with a potato peeler or knife, then cut it into 2cm/¾in cubes. Put these in a large bowl, add the salt and toss well.

2 Cut the chillies in half, scrape out the seeds with a sharp knife, then cut the flesh into fine strips. Grate the rind of one of the limes thinly, removing only the coloured part of the skin, then cut the lime in half and squeeze the juice.

3 Add the chillies, lime rind and juice to the *jicama* and mix thoroughly to ensure that all the *jicama* cubes are coated. Cut the other lime into wedges.

4 Cover and chill for at least 1 hour before serving with lime wedges. If the salad is to be served as an appetizer with drinks, transfer the *jicama* cubes to little bowls and offer them with cocktail sticks for spearing.

INDEX